BOLLINGEN SERIES LXI

ERICH NEUMANN

# Art and the Creative
# Unconscious

FOUR ESSAYS

*Translated from the German by*
Ralph Manheim

BOLLINGEN SERIES LXI

PRINCETON UNIVERSITY PRESS

Copyright © 1959, by Bollingen Foundation Inc.
Published by Princeton University Press, Princeton, N.J.

*Second hardcover printing,
with bibliographical revisions, 1969
Third hardcover printing, 1972*

First Princeton/Bollingen Paperback Edition, 1971

*Third printing, 1974*

THIS IS THE SIXTY-FIRST PUBLICATION IN A SERIES OF
WORKS SPONSORED BY BOLLINGEN FOUNDATION
*Library of Congress Catalogue Card No. 58-8984*
ISBN 0-691-01773-5 (paperback edn.)
ISBN 0-691-09706-2 (hardcover edn.)

MANUFACTURED IN THE UNITED STATES OF AMERICA

Princeton University Press books are printed on acid-free paper
and meet the guidelines for permanence and durability of the
Committee on Production Guidelines for Book Longevity of the
Council on Library Resources

9   11   13   15   14   12   10

# EDITORIAL NOTE

The present volume is a translation of *Kunst und schöpfer-isches Unbewusstes,* which was published in 1954 by Rascher Verlag, Zurich, as the third of a series of volumes of collected essays by Erich Neumann under the common title "Umkreisung der Mitte." To the three original essays a fourth has been added.

The first essay, on Leonardo da Vinci, has been considerably revised for this edition. The second, "Art and Time," was previously published in *Eranos-Jahrbuch 1951* (Zurich); in the present translation it appeared in *Man and Time* (Papers from the Eranos Yearbooks, 3; New York [Bollingen Series XXX], 1957, and London, 1958). The fourth, "Creative Man and Transformation," was previously published only in *Eranos-Jahrbuch 1954.*

Acknowledgment is gratefully made to the Hogarth Press, London, for permission to quote poetry of Rilke in the Cruikshank and Leishman-Spender translations; to Oxford University Press, London, for permission to quote from Irma A. Richter's selections from the Notebooks of Leonardo; and to Jonathan Cape, London, for permission to quote from Edward MacCurdy's edition of the Notebooks. Grateful acknowledgment is also made to J. M. Cohen and Ruth Speirs for the use of their unpublished translations of Rilke. Figure 1 and certain quotations are from Freud's essay on Leonardo da Vinci in Vol. XI of the Standard Edition of the Complete Psychological Works of Sigmund Freud, published by Hogarth Press, London, and The Macmillan Co., New York.

# CONTENTS

# LIST OF ILLUSTRATIONS

Plates

*following page 100*

Text Figures

ART AND THE CREATIVE
UNCONSCIOUS

# I

## LEONARDO DA VINCI
## AND THE MOTHER ARCHETYPE

In any attempt to come closer to the personality of
Leonardo da Vinci, it will be well to bear in mind the
words of Jakob Burckhardt: "The colossal outlines of
Leonardo's nature can never be more than dimly and dis-
tantly conceived." [1] And yet this towering figure, great
artist and great scientist in one, will always represent a
challenge: What was the mysterious force that made
such a phenomenon possible?

Neither Leonardo's scientific interests nor his versatility were unique in the age of the Renaissance when the
world was being newly discovered; but even next to the
many-sided Leon Battista Alberti, as Burckhardt said,
"Leonardo da Vinci was as the finisher to the beginner, as
the master to the dilettante." [2] Yet although, in addition
to his writings about art, Leonardo arrived at fundamental insights about the nature of science and experimenta-
tion; although he discovered important laws of mechanics and hydraulics, geology and paleontology; although

1. Jakob Burckhardt, *The Civilization of the Renaissance in
Italy*, p. 87. [For full references, see the List of Works Cited.]
2. Ibid., p. 87.

as an engineer he may be said to have anticipated the discovery of the airplane and the submarine; although he not only studied the anatomy and physiology of the human body, but perhaps, through his comparative anatomy of man and animal, was the first of thinkers to grasp the unity of organic development—what fascinates us more than all these impressive individual achievements, each one of which has been surpassed in the course of the centuries, is the unsurpassable individuality of Leonardo the man, which extends into an area of human existence that is beyond time and in human measure eternal.

As a Western phenomenon, Leonardo fascinates us very much in the same way as Goethe, precisely because we here encounter a striving for a life of individuation, a life of wholeness, which seems to be in keeping with the intimate intention of Western humanity.

We owe the first basic attempt to understand Leonardo by means of depth psychology to Sigmund Freud, who in his essay *Leonardo da Vinci and A Memory of His Childhood,* which was written in 1910, took up certain essential problems of Leonardo's psychology. The present work will embody a different approach, based on the analytical psychology of C. G. Jung, which, unlike the personalistic psychology of Freud, starts from transpersonal, archetypal factors.

Whereas Freud attempts to derive Leonardo's psychology from the personal events of his childhood—i.e., from a mother complex created by his family circumstances—we find a fundamental, not a pathological, phenomenon in the dominance of the mother archetype, i.e., of a

4

suprapersonal mother image, in the creative man. It is revealing in this connection that Freud, unconsciously no doubt, distorted Leonardo's family circumstances in a manner consonant with his theory, but that on the other hand, precisely in this study, he penetrated to the transpersonal process underlying Leonardo's development, broadening "the basis of this analysis by a comparative study of the historical material." [3] But he drew no consequences from all this.

Leonardo was born in 1452, the illegitimate son of a notary, Ser Piero da Vinci, and of a peasant girl "of good family." [4] Freud's personalistic derivation of Leonardo's psychology is based on the assumption that Leonardo spent the first (and, in Freud's view, decisive) years of his life as a fatherless child with his mother Caterina. [5] The facts, however, were quite different. "After 1452 Piero made a marriage appropriate to his class, and shortly afterward Caterina did likewise." [6] The child Leonardo grew up with his father and stepmother in his grandfather's house, where the whole family was living together in 1457. [7] Since legitimate children were born to Leonardo's father only in 1472, in his third marriage, Leonardo lived as an only child with his grandmother

3. C. G. Jung, *Symbols of Transformation*, par. 3.
4. Marie Herzfeld (ed.), *Leonardo da Vinci, der Denker, Forscher und Poet.*
5. Freud, *Leonardo da Vinci* (Standard Edn.), p. 91.
6. Herzfeld, introduction.
7. We happen to have documentary proof of this family life for the year 1457, but of course this does not mean that Leonardo was taken into the family only at this time, as Freud (p. 91) supposes.

and successively with two childless stepmothers. We know nothing of any meetings with his real mother. But in any event the family circumstances are very complicated, sufficiently so to provide a basis for all sorts of contradictory psychological constructions.

But even though all the psychological consequences that Freud drew from a false personalistic approach are thus annulled, he did not stop here; for in an extremely penetrating way he made Leonardo's childhood recollection, i.e., an unquestionable document of Leonardo's psychic reality, into a broader foundation of his work. This childhood recollection, the so-called "vulture fantasy," is to be found among Leonardo's notes on the flight of birds, particularly vultures. It runs as follows: "It seems that I was always destined to be so deeply concerned with vultures; for I recall as one of my very earliest memories that while I was in my cradle a vulture came down to me, and opened my mouth with its tail, and struck me many times with its tail against my lips." [8]

It is striking that so critical a man as Leonardo should have recorded this recollection as something perfectly self-evident; he did not make the reservation that Freud unhesitatingly adopts in speaking of the "vulture fantasy." The very fact that Leonardo, despite the critical "mi parea" ("it seemed to me"), speaks of this event as an actual childhood memory demonstrates the psychic

8. "Questo scriver si distintamente del nibio par che sia mio destino, perchè nella mia prima recordatione della mia infanta e' mi parea che, essendo io in culla, che un nibio venissi a me e mi aprissi la bocca colla sua coda e molte volte mi percuotesse con tal coda dentro alle labbra." Codex Atlanticus, fol. 65ᵛ; Freud, p. 82.

reality of his experience. The child—and the smaller he is, the more intensely so—lives in a prepersonal world, i.e., a world essentially conditioned by the archetypes, a world whose unity is not yet, as in a developed consciousness, split into an outward physical reality and an inward psychic reality. Consequently, everything that happens to his still undeveloped personality has a numinous, mythical character, a fateful significance like the intervention of the divine.[9] In this sense Leonardo's "naïve," unreflecting record shows that his recollection deals with a fundamental event, a central motif in his existence, and that if we can understand it we shall have arrived at a hidden but decisive aspect of his life.

But before we go into the interpretation of this fantasy and its significance for Leonardo in Freud's view and our own, we must say a few words about Freud's so-called "mistake." It was pointed out recently [10] that the bird mentioned by Leonardo, the *nibio* or *nibbio,* is not a vulture but a kite. And the question rises: to what extent does this destroy the foundations of Freud's study and of our own that is partly based on it?

Freud's "mistake" in taking the bird for a vulture led him to the mother-significance of the vulture in Egypt, and the symbolic equation *vulture = mother* provided

9. Cf. Rudolf Otto, "Spontanes Erwachen des sensus numinis," and Ernst Barlach's childhood memories in *Ein selbsterzähltes Leben.*

10. Irma A. Richter (ed.), in a footnote to her *Selections from the Notebooks of Leonardo da Vinci* (1952), p. 286; Ernest Jones, *The Life and Work of Sigmund Freud,* Vol. II (1955), p. 390; James Strachey, editorial note to Freud, Vol. XI (1957), pp. 59 ff.

the basis for his understanding of Leonardo's childhood fantasy, for his unsubstantiated theory about Leonardo's relation to his personal mother, and for the mother fixation by which he explained Leonardo's development. "The phantasy and the myth," writes Strachey, the able editor of Freud's works, "seem to have no immediate connection with each other." [11] Nevertheless he argues against the reader's possible impulse "to dismiss the whole study as worthless." [12]

As we shall see, Freud's "mistake" is by no means so damaging to his study, much less to our own, as one might at first suppose. On the contrary, our critique of Freud's study and our attempt to substitute a transpersonal interpretation for his personalistic derivation of the fantasy from Leonardo's relation to his personal mother are actually confirmed by the discovery of this error. Even if the bird is not a vulture, i.e., a bird whose mother-significance is mythologically established, but some other bird, the basic element of the fantasy is preserved, namely the movement of the bird's tail between the infant's lips.

Birds in general are symbols of the spirit and soul. The bird symbol may be male as well as female; when it makes its appearance, we know nothing of its sex, except in the case of birds of definite symbolic sexuality, such as the eagle—male—or the vulture—female.

But the real basis of any interpretation is the bird's action in Leonardo's childhood fantasy. In connection with the infant lying in his cradle, the bird's tail is primarily

11. Ibid., p. 62.    12. Ibid., p. 61.

a symbol of the maternal breast; but at the same time Freud correctly interpreted it as the male genital organ. From this basic constellation emerging in the childhood memory, he attempted to derive both the personal mother complex of the fatherless Leonardo and a passively homosexual tendency in his love life. Both derivations are false and require a correction, since the "vulture fantasy" is a transpersonal, archetypal constellation, and not one that may be derived personalistically from Leonardo's family romance.

In the situation of the babe drinking at the maternal breast, the mother always represents also the uroboric, i.e., male-female, greatness of the mother in relation to the child she bears, nourishes, and protects. In this function, her lifegiving breasts—as may be demonstrated in primitive sculpture, for example—often become phallic symbols, in relation to which the child takes the attitude of receiving and conceiving. This is a fundamental human situation with nothing perverse or abnormal about it; and in this situation the child, whether male or female, is feminine and conceiving, while the maternal is male and fecundating. The suprapersonal character of this experience for Leonardo is made clear by the fact that in his recollection the personal mother is meaningfully replaced by the bird symbol.

We call a unity of this sort "uroboric," because the uroboros, the circular snake eating its tail, is the symbol of the "Great Round," which, circling round itself, begetting and bearing, is male and female at once.[13]

13. See my *Origins and History of Consciousness*, pp. 8–13.

This uroboros, whose hieroglyph in Egypt is interpreted as universe,[14] embraces heaven, water, earth, and stars, i.e., all the elements as well as old age and renewal; in alchemy it is still the symbol of the primordial unity that contains the opposites. This is what makes the uroboros so eminently appropriate a symbol by which to represent the early psychic state in which consciousness is not yet separate from the unconscious, with all the decisive psychic consequences that this situation embraces for the relation of the ego to the unconscious and of man to the world.

Therefore, even if the bird in Leonardo's childhood fantasy is not a vulture but some other bird, it remains a symbol of the uroboric Great Mother, with whom we must associate not only the feminine symbolism of the nurturing breasts, but also the male symbolism of the fecundating phallus. Thus the image of the uroboric mother does not result from a mistaken notion of the little boy concerning his mother's genitals, but is a symbolic representation of the Archetypal Feminine as the creative source of life, which is alive in the unconscious of every human being regardless of sex.

Here we must go into some detail regarding the archetype of the maternal kite-vulture. As Jung has shown, such archetypes can also emerge spontaneously, i.e., independently of any historical or archaeological knowledge, in the dreams and fantasies of modern men.[15] In

14. George Boas (tr. and ed.), *The Hieroglyphics of Horapollo*, p. 57.

15. Cf. the works of Jung and his followers on the spontaneous emergence of the archetypes in children, normal persons, psychopaths, and sufferers from mental disorders.

original, primitive mankind, to whom the connection between sexuality and childbearing was still unknown, the feminine—as is still shown by totemism, with its descent from animals, plants, elements—was fecundated by a transpersonal male principle that appeared as spirit or godhead, as ancestor or wind, but never in the form of a concrete personal man. In this sense, the woman was "autonomous," i.e., a virgin dependent on no earthly male. She was the numinous conceiver, the numinous author of life, father and mother in one.

But the outstanding representatives of this archetype of the Great Mother are the Great Goddesses of Egypt, whose chief symbol is the vulture which Freud, "by mistake," substituted for the "more innocuous" bird of Leonardo's fantasy. Yet in all likelihood this "blunder" on the part of a man so conscientious as Freud is explained by his preoccupation with Leonardo's fantasy, which, despite his personalistic view and interpretation, seems to have activated the archetypal image of the Great Mother within him.[16] In support of this contention it might be remarked that in this study, which he first, oddly enough, published anonymously, Freud drew on mythological, archetypal material in a way quite unusual for him. He pointed out that the vulture goddess Mut, identical with Nekhbet, was often represented phallically in Egypt.[17] The androgynous Great Mother

16. There is no contradiction between this possibility and Strachey's explanation that Freud found *"nibio"* translated as *"Geier"* (vulture) in many of his German sources.

17. Lanzone, *Dizionario di mitologia egizia,* Pls. cxxxvi–cxxxviii.

Goddess, i.e., equipped with a phallus and sometimes a beard, is a universally distributed archetype symbolizing the unity of the creative in the primordial creatrix, the "parthenogenetic" matriarchal Mother Goddess of the beginning. This fundamental view of matriarchal psychology, the importance of which we have repeatedly stressed,[18] expressed itself in Egypt in the belief that vultures, which were all thought to be female, conceived by the wind.

The vulture goddess Nekhbet with the white crown, the reigning goddess of Upper Egypt, is the representative of an ancient matriarchal stratum. She was the mother of the king, and even in late times hovered protectively over his head, while the queen's vulture hood indicated her ancient rank. In Egypt the word "mother" was written with the sign of the vulture, which is the symbol of the goddess Mut, the original "Great Mother." As a devourer of corpses, the vulture is also the Terrible Mother, who takes the dead back into herself; as "she with the outspread wings," the vulture was the sheltering symbol of heaven, of the generative and food-giving Goddess, who generates the lights, the sun, moon, and stars, out of her motherly nocturnal darkness. For this reason the vulture goddess was called Eileithyia by the Greeks, i.e., equated with the Mother Goddess who helped in childbirth—a figure encompassing the pre-Hellenic Cretan Mother Goddess, the many-breasted Artemis of Asia Minor, as well as Hera and the Demeter of the Eleusinian mysteries. The Goddess

18. Cf. my *Zur Psychologie des Weiblichen*, a volume of essays devoted to that theme.

and the queen representing her ruled over life, fertility, heaven, and earth. The Egyptian king, her son, says characteristically of himself: I am descended "from those my two mothers, the vulture with long hair and exuberant breasts, up on Mount Sehseh; may she set her breast to my mouth and never wean me." [19] "Never weaned": the grown king is represented sitting in the lap of the Mother Goddess—Mut, Hathor, or Isis—drinking from her breasts. And this symbolism is of decisive importance for our context.

The vulture goddess of the rain, from whose fruitful breasts, in the case of the Egyptian Nut, for example, the fecundating moisture flows, gives the masculine earth to drink—as Isis suckles King Horus. As Great Goddess she is male-female, fecundating and childbearing, in one.

For this reason the vulture goddess Nekhbet was worshiped as a "form of the primeval abyss which brought forth the light," [20] and her name was "The father of fathers, the mother of mothers, who hath existed from the beginning and is the creatrix of the world."

Against the background of these archetypal relations, the bird of Leonardo's childhood fantasy, considered in its creative-uroboric unity of breast-mother and phallus-father, is symbolically a "vulture" even if Leonardo called it a *"nibio."* For only if we penetrate the symbolic, archetypal significance of the fantasy can we understand

19. Kurt Heinrich Sethe (ed.), *Die alt-aegyptischen Pyramidentexte,* Pyr. 1116/19.

20. E. A. W. Budge, *The Gods of the Egyptians,* Vol. I, p. 440. This watery abyss is the heavenly water of the night sea in its unity of upper and lower world, as will be discussed elsewhere.

this bird and what it does. Whether with Freud we take Leonardo's "reminiscence" as a "fantasy" or with others term it a "dream," we are referring to symbolic action in a psychic area, not to the physical action of a zoological specimen in a geographically definable locality.

For this reason we are perfectly justified in retaining the term "vulture" which Freud chose "by mistake," for it was through this very "blunder" that his keen intuition penetrated to the core of the matter, even though he did not fully understand and interpret it. For no zoologically definable bird, no "kite" or "vulture," is uroboric and behaves like Leonardo's bird. But such behavior is perfectly plausible for the "vulture" as symbol of the uroboric Mother, which lived in the psyche of the Egyptians as of Leonardo [21]—and of Freud.

The symbolism of the bird and its male-phallic components accent the spirit aspect of this archetype in contrast to its earth aspect. In Egypt we know the nutritive cow of heaven also as a symbol of the nurturing Great Mother. Yet in the paradoxical symbolism of the "vulture with the exuberant breasts," the accent is on the heavenly nature of this bird, which shelters the earth with its wings. But bird–heaven–wind are archetypal spirit symbols that are also characteristic of the father archetype. Above and below, heaven and earth, are contained in the father-mother unity of the uroboros and the uroboric Mother. The spirit character of this Mother is

21. Possibly this phenomenon provides the answer to another "riddle" with which we shall be concerned below, namely the "picture-puzzle" of a vulture discovered by Pfister in one of Leonardo's paintings. See below, pp. 63 f.

expressed by the bird—just as her earth character is expressed by the snake symbol.

If we know that the bird in Leonardo's childhood fantasy relates not to the father but to the uroboric Great Mother, it is only because it appeared in the earliest phase of human life, to an infant lying in his cradle, for this is the phase of the Mother with her nourishing or phallic breasts. In an older child, a similar experience of a bird, e.g., the rape of Ganymede by the eagle of Zeus, would have an entirely different meaning.

The "kite," to be sure, calls for a new correction of Freud's study. But this correction consists in still stronger emphasis on the impossibility of a personalistic interpretation, i.e., an interpretation on the basis of Leonardo's family history and relation to his actual mother. Not only has the transpersonal, archetypal interpretation of Leonardo and the creative process in general been confirmed, but we see that it must be carried to new depths. Another shift of accent necessitated by the discovery of Freud's error (in which we had partly followed him) is to lend new emphasis to the uroboric character of Leonardo's "vulture mother."

Here we cannot take up the whole scope of what the Archetypal Feminine means to mankind,[22] but we must give at least some idea of it. It appears both as the all-generative aspect of nature and as the creative source of the unconscious, from which consciousness was born in the course of human history, and out of which unceasingly, in all times and in every man, there arise

22. Cf. my *Great Mother*.

new psychic contents that broaden, intensify, and enrich the life of the individual and of the community. In this sense the prayer to the Mother Goddess, "May she set her breast to my mouth and never wean me," is valid for all men, but most particularly for the creative man.

Nevertheless the question remains: In cases where this archetypal image is dominant, when are we dealing with a mother complex—i.e., a pathological, "infantile" mother fixation that makes healthy life impossible, especially for a male—and when with a legitimate and genuine archetypal situation? In this sketch devoted specially to Leonardo, we have space only to suggest certain contexts that will be discussed elsewhere in detail.

With the development of consciousness the male-female uroborus becomes differentiated into the First Parents. In the matriarchal phase of human history, and in child development, where the unconscious is preponderant, the First Parents are constellated as the uroboric Virgin Mother in union with the invisible Spirit Father, who is the paternal uroboros, an anonymous transpersonal spiritual being.[23] In normal development a "secondary personalization" takes place, i.e., a process of demythicization, in which the archetypally mythological images are projected upon the persons of the family or the immediate environment and experienced through them. This process leads to the formation of a normal personality and of a "normal" relation to the outside world. The archetypes are gradually transferred to the "cultural canon" recognized by the community in ques-

23. See my *Origins and History*, p. 18.

tion and in this way the individual is adapted to normal life. The archetypal tension between Spirit Father and Virgin Mother is reduced in this development to a tension between consciousness, which by way of the patriarchal world comes into the inheritance of the Spirit Father, and the unconscious, which becomes the living representative of the Great Mother. Normal Western development, which for this reason we call patriarchal, leads to a dominance of consciousness or of the father archetype, and to an extensive repression and inhibition of the unconscious and the related mother archetype. But in the creative man—and to a considerable degree in the neurotic—this reduction of the archetypal tension between the First Parents is impossible or incomplete.

In the creative man we find a preponderance of the archetypal in keeping with his creative nature; in the sick man we find a disturbance of the normal development of consciousness, caused in part by the constellations of the family and in part by genuine childhood experiences—or else the factors making for sickness may arise at later stages of development.

The consequences of this accentuation of the archetype in the creative man, who by his very nature is dependent on his receptivity toward the creative unconscious, manifest themselves partly in deviations from the development of the so-called normal man; here we need not deal with the somewhat similar condition of the neurotic. In the life of the creative man the emphasis always lies on the transpersonal factors; i.e., in his experience the archetypal factor is so predominant that in extreme cases he becomes almost incapable of personal relations. But even where he retains his capacity for human contact and human relations, it is always at the price of an essential conflict that he assimilates the archetypal projections and does justice to the human limitations of his counterpart. And this is why many artists, even among the most gifted, have such intense anima relations with the "distant loved one," epistolary relations, relations to the unknown, the dead, etc.

In normal development, the man's "feminine component" is largely repressed and contributes to the constellation of the anima [24] in the unconscious, which, projected upon the woman, makes contact with her possible. But in the creative man this process is incomplete. By his very nature he remains in high degree bisexual, and the retained feminine component is manifested by his increased "receptivity," by his sensibility and a greater emphasis in his life on the "matriarchal consciousness," [25] expressed in inward processes of parturition and formation that essentially condition his creativeness.

Nor does the anima develop in the same way as in the normal man. As we have elsewhere shown, it is the patriarchal, masculine development of consciousness that conditions the constellation of the anima figure and its differentiation from the mother archetype.[26] In the creative man this differentiation cannot be fully effected; the creative man lacks the requisite one-sidedness that

24. Jung, "The Relations between the Ego and the Unconscious," pars. 296 ff.
25. See my *Psychologie des Weiblichen.*
26. See my *Origins and History,* p. 198.

marks ego-identification with the purely masculine consciousness, for he remains both more childlike and more womanly than the normal man. The preponderance of the archetypal world of the Great Mother, his dependence on her "exuberant breasts," are so strong that he is never capable of the "matricide" necessary for the liberation of the anima. For this reason the creative man—except in his supreme representatives—is usually less a man than a creator. Precisely in the measure of his ability to assimilate and give form to the contents of the unconscious that are lacking in the community in which he lives, he is incapable of developing himself as an individual in relation to the community.[27] Whereas the normal man to a great extent pays for his adaptation to life in Western civilization with a loss of creativity, the creative man, who is adapted to the requirements of the unconscious world, pays for his creativity with loneliness, which is the expression of his relative lack of adaptation to the life of the community. Of course this characterization applies only to the extreme positions, between which an endless number of transitions and shadings are possible.

In any event the creative man is very largely fixated in the matriarchal stage of the psyche, and, like the Egyptian king, he experiences himself as the archetypal hero-son of the Virgin Mother, who "never weans" him. Thus Leonardo as "vulture child" is a typical hero-son and fulfills the archetypal canon of the hero's birth, which we have elsewhere discussed at length.

27. See the next essay in this volume.

"The fact that the hero has two fathers and two mothers is a central feature in the canon of the hero myth. Besides his personal father there is a 'higher,' that is to say an archetypal, father figure, and similarly an archetypal mother figure appears beside the personal mother. . . .

"As A. Jeremias [28] has pointed out and amply proved, the essence of the mythological canon of the hero-redeemer is that he is fatherless or motherless, that one of the parents is often divine, and that the hero's mother is frequently the Mother Goddess herself or else betrothed to a god." [29]

Leonardo's bird mother is the Mother Goddess herself; she is the "god's betrothed," impregnated by the "wind," one of the archetypal symbols of the Spirit Father, but at the same time she is the phallic, uroboric Mother who begets and gives birth to herself. In this sense Leonardo, like all heroes, had "two" mothers, and experienced himself as the son not of a personal but of an "unknown" father, or else was "fatherless." [30]

The relation to the Great Mother determines the childhood and youth of the hero; in this period he lives as her son-lover, favored by the fullness of her devotion and endangered by her dominance. Psychologically speaking, this means that the development and unfolding of his ego consciousness and his personality are largely gov-

28. *Handbuch der altorientalischen Geisteskultur,* pp. 205 ff.
29. See my *Origins and History,* pp. 132–33.
30. As we know, the childlike notion of being a "stepchild," i.e., not the real child of the father or mother, is found in many neurotics, but not only in neurotics.

erned by processes in which the unconscious plays a more important part than the ego.

In the course of the patriarchal development of consciousness, the bond with the Great Mother is broken, and after the dragon fight the hero is reborn into a relation with the Spirit Father; he fulfills his mythological task as one twice born.

Dragon fight and "slaying of the parents" mean the surpassing of the "mother" as the symbol of an unconscious that holds the son fast in the collective world of drives; and they signify also the surpassing of the "father," symbol of the collective values and traditions of his time. Only after this victory does the hero achieve his own new world, the world of his individual mission, in which the figures of the uroboric parents, of the mother and father archetype, assume a new aspect. They are no longer hostile, confining powers, but companions, bestowing their blessings on the life and work of the victorious hero-son.

The Great Individual, the creative man, must travel this archetypally determined way in the manner appropriate to his individuality, his time, and his mission. But although the terms "hero" and "dragon fight" apply to this type of career, another form of the Great Individual's development may take a different course.

One group of Great Individuals with their dramatic careers pursues the way of the hero; we have only to think of Michelangelo or Beethoven. But there are other careers that rather take the form of a slow development, of a gradual inner growth. Although dramatic crises and phases are not lacking in these developments, in the life of Goethe, for example, here one has more the impression of a steady, almost imperceptible being-led than of conscious heroic action.[31] The first development corresponds to a patriarchal development in opposition to the Great Mother, and the heroes reborn in the dragon fight prove themselves sons of the Spirit Father. The other type of heroic development is clearly more matriarchal, i.e., closer to the mother archetype.

In both cases the mythological constellation of the hero's birth and childlike, youthlike relation to the Great Mother Goddess stands at the beginning of the development. But whereas the patriarchal heroes leave the Great Mother and in opposition to her must prove themselves sons of the Spirit Father, the life of the matriarchal heroes is continuously dominated by the Mother and never wholly departs from the shelter of her spirit wings.

Although a preponderance of the transpersonal archetypal world may be demonstrated in all Great Individuals, it makes a great difference in their life development whether, when the First Parents separate, it is the archetype of the Virgin Mother or of the Spirit Father that remains dominant.[32]

A one-sided development, in which the one or the other archetype is exclusively dominant and there is no compensation by its complement, represents an extreme

31. Here one is involuntarily reminded of Schiller's distinction between "naïve" and "sentimental" writing in "Über naive und sentimentale Dichtung," though in this connection it cannot be reduced to the opposing types of attitude developed in Jung's *Psychological Types*.

32. Here we need not discuss the different meanings that these constellations may assume in masculine and feminine psychology.

psychic danger.[33] But in the Great Individuals we always find that although one of the First Parents, either the Great Mother or the Great Father, sets his stamp on their destiny, the other member also exerts an important influence on the course of their development.

In the career of the patriarchal hero, the hero reborn as son of the Spirit Father ultimately returns to a relationship with the archetype of the Great Mother. His heroic career begins with his conquest of her, but ultimately—as in the case of Herakles and Hera—the original conflict is resolved in his reconciliation with her. Similarly, the Great Individual whose life is stamped by the dominance of the Archetypal Feminine must, in the course of his development, come to grips with the Spirit Father. Only in the tension between the archetypal worlds of the Great Mother and the Great Father is the wholeness of a truly creative existence fulfilled. But the individual mode of development, of life and work, will be determined by whether the hero-son takes a predominantly patriarchal or matriarchal, solar or lunar, course; by whether the patriarchal and matriarchal aspects of his consciousness are relatively balanced or in a relation of tension to one another.

It can be demonstrated in many cases that these decisive constellations of the archetypal world are often manifested in the dreams, fantasies, or memories of early

33. This danger is manifested in neurosis and psychosis. It takes the form of matriarchal or patriarchal "castration," the overpowering of the individual by the maternally uroboric nature of the unconscious, or by the equally menacing paternally uroboric nature of the spirit. (Cf. my *Origins and History,* index, s. vv.)

childhood. Precisely because the child, with its undeveloped consciousness, still lives in the mythical world of the primordial images and like early man has a "mythological apperception" of the world, the impressions of this period, in which the profoundest strata can be expressed or rather "imagined" without falsification, seem to anticipate the whole life.

Such "image-inations" take the form of childhood memories or fantasies.[34] In this sense Leonardo's childhood memory strikes the dominant chord of his life; it is a meaningful symbol of the fact that his life would be dominated by the vulture goddess, the Great Mother.

It is hard to judge to what extent Leonardo's actual family situation favored the projection of his archetypal hero situation. We may safely assume that there was little intimacy between him and his father. The notary was an extremely worldly and active man; aside from the illegitimate relation to Leonardo's mother he contracted no less than four legitimate marriages. But by his third and fourth marriages—when he married for the third time he was already forty-five years of age—he had nine sons and two daughters. If to this biography we compare the life of Leonardo—who, except perhaps in his youth,[35] had no known physical relations with any woman—and if we consider that Leonardo, despite his fame, was treated by his father as an "illegitimate son"

34. In his seminars on the dreams of children at the Technische Hochschule in Zurich, Jung expressed decisive insights regarding the life-determining character of childhood dreams. (Unpublished.)

35. Cf. his attitude toward sexuality and the "desires," pp. 28 ff.

and not even mentioned in his will, it does not seem far-fetched to assume that there was a basic antagonism between father and son. Besides this alienation from his personal father, this man so arrogant in his worldliness as to disinherit his "illegitimate son," we must consider the problematic relation of the child Leonardo to women, to his grandmother, his two stepmothers, and to his own mother, whom he may or may not have known.

Even in the average child such abnormal family situations usually lead to disorders: as a result of a compensatory excitation of the unconscious, the parent archetypes are not "abolished," as in normal development, and the great suprapersonal parents compensate in a sense for the absence or insufficiency of the personal parents.[36]

When we take into account Leonardo's creative predisposition, with its "natural" preponderance of the archetypal, his childhood fantasy becomes understandable as a symbol of his detachment from the normal human environment and of his relation to the transpersonal powers with all their fateful meaning. And what makes Leonardo's "vulture fantasy" so significant a document is precisely that the same archetypal constellations and symbols that were related concerning the mythical heroes of prehistory should appear in a man of the Western Renaissance.

Even as a young man—insofar as we are able to form a picture of him—Leonardo was characterized by the inability to tie himself down to any one preoccupation

36. The disturbances in normal adaptation brought about by this compensation need not concern us here.

that distinguished him throughout his lifetime. Even for a period when versatility was almost the rule, his many-sidedness is amazing. For in addition to his genius as a painter, which stood out so clearly when he was a boy studying under Verocchio that his master is said to have given up painting on his account,[37] the youthful Leonardo seems to have fascinated all those about him by the abundance of his talents.

Up to his old age Leonardo was uncommonly beautiful, combining charm and elegance with extraordinary physical strength; he could bend a horseshoe with his bare hands. He was a playful child of the Muses, known for his ability to sing, write poetry, play musical instruments, and improvise music. His outstanding mathematical and technical gifts made him famous in his time as a hydraulic and military engineer, a builder of fortresses, and an inventor; and these gifts too he employed in a characteristically playful way.[38] He was called to the court of Milan, for example, not as a famous painter but because he had invented an odd musical instrument shaped like a horse's head. Even as an old man he continued to devise strange toys and enlivened the court festivities of many princes with all sorts of technical

37. Giorgio Vasari, *The Lives of the Painters,* Vol. III, p. 222.
38. Two hundred of his inventions were constructed in the twentieth century by the Italian government and shown in an exhibition. (See *Life* magazine, July 17, 1939.) Machine gun, parachute, fire ladder, steam engine, telescope, printing press, roll press, drill, windmill, propeller, steering gear, and many other inventions, as well as instruments such as a step counter, a wind measurer, and innumerable others (F. M. Feldhaus, *Leonardo der Techniker und Erfinder*) are among the products of his technical genius.

games and inventions that strike us as unworthy of his genius. From the very start he was more preoccupied with the inventiveness and inexhaustible fertility of his own nature than with the shaping of a reality which in a sense he never in all his lifetime took quite seriously. He moved through his time and world—painting, sculpturing, experimenting, discovering, and inventing, profoundly interested in all these pursuits—yet always uncommitted, always independent, always an outsider, never giving himself entirely to anything or anyone, except to his own nature, whose dictates he obeyed as though in a dream, but at the same time with the sharpened alertness of a scientific observer.

"To devise," he writes, "is the work of the master, to execute the act of the servant." [39] One might be tempted to regard this as the motto of his fragmentary work and of his life. But unjustly so. In his youth, perhaps, his unwillingness to tie himself down may at times have involved him in the arrogance that merely plans but never executes. In reality he was a stupendous worker, except that, for reasons the investigation of which is one of our main tasks, he never strove to build up an "opus" such as that of Michelangelo, who in his hard one-sidedness despised him for this.

The fragmentary tendency in his art was not based on indifference regarding execution, nor did it spring wholly from the vastness of his inward image. It was

39. MS. C.A., fol. 109. See Herzfeld, p. 139; for the abbreviations etc., see p. clxvi, or Richter, *Selections,* p. 393. English version in Edward MacCurdy, *The Notebooks of Leonardo da Vinci,* Vol. I, p. 95.

also an expression of the fact that the work of art, and art itself, were not for him an end in themselves but only —though perhaps he himself was not aware of it—an instrument and expression of his inner situation. In this, as in his fascination with the problem of flying, to which he devoted so much energy and passion, Leonardo showed himself to be a "vulture child." At heart he despised reality and its tasks; he despised money and fame, the opus, the establishment of a school, for in his unconscious devotion to the Spirit Mother he was profoundly alien to everything material and matter of fact. This was also the reason for his aversion to the instinctual urges and his rejection of sexuality. "The ermine will die rather than besmirch itself," [40] runs one of his aphorisms. And another: "The man who does not restrain wantonness allies himself with beasts." [41] And, concluding a banal allegory about a butterfly that comes to grief after being attracted by the radiant beauty of the light, he moralizes in true medieval style: "This applies to those who, when they see before them carnal and worldly delights, hasten to them like the butterfly without ever taking thought as to their nature, which they will learn to know to their shame and loss." [42] The in-

40. MS. H. I, fol. 48ᵛ. See Herzfeld, p. 143; Richter, *Selections,* p. 319. [The quotations and ms. citations are mainly from the latter volume, though page citations are given to both presentations of the *Notebooks.*—Ed.]

41. MS. H. III, fol. 119ʳ. See Herzfeld, p. 140; *Selections,* p. 280.

42. MS. C.A., fol. 257ʳ. See Herzfeld, pp. 270–71; *Selections,* p. 243.

volved translation does justice to Leonardo's own suddenly halting and stammering expression.

Unquestionably there was in Leonardo a strong sexual block, a kind of sexual anxiety, but this rejection extended to the whole material side of reality and life. As we have seen, the uroboric Great Mother has also phallic, procreative, masculine, paternal features, in relation to which—to the phallic breasts, for example—the child is receptive and "feminine." In the same sense, the creative man is "feminine" in his passive openness to the creative flow. Accordingly, we have termed this attitude of the personality and consciousness "matriarchal." Here we need not decide whether the predominance of passive-feminine or active-masculine traits in the creative life of the individual is brought about by constitutional factors or by the events of his life. It seems likely that such constellations affect the relationship between activity and passivity, between masculine and feminine elements, not only in the individual's psychic life but also in his relation to his own and the opposite sex. In any event the ultimate sexual attitude of the personality is determined not by a single factor but by many, not by a single developmental constellation, such as an orientation toward the "Great Mother," but by a number of such constellations and phases. Thus the bond with the uroboric Great Mother is characteristic of many creative men who show no sign of homosexuality.

Another typical constellation of symbolic homosexual attachment is that of the young lovers—in whom the accent is precisely not on openness toward the masculine aspect of the Great Mother, but on resistance to it. We often find such a resistance in the "young sons" of the Great Mother, who in their hypersensitive budlikeness reject life; supposing life to be "meaningless," they are actually for the most part unequal to it. His by no means proved homosexuality—in any case, his homoeroticism— fits into this context. As in many young lovers of the Great Mother, compensatory resistance to her aspect as Earth Mother, as matter, favored a tendency toward male association and toward a rejection of the beauty of the feminine, which fetters the passions and binds one to the commonplace reality of matter. If Leonardo, as alleged, selected his pupils more for their beauty than for their talent, this is quite in keeping with his nature, in which Eros played so crucial a role, and with his devotion to the purposeless beauty of living things, which meant more to him than any opus or school. The actual aim and motive of his central actions can always be shown to lie in something "transcending the real."

There is no doubt that in studying the flight of birds and the mechanics of their wings, in his tireless efforts to build a flying machine, Leonardo was striving very concretely to acquire the technique of flight for mankind. "The great bird will take its first flight from the back of a giant swan," he wrote. "It will fill the universe with wonder; all writings will be full of its fame, bringing eternal glory to the place of its origin." [43] This famous sentence is usually taken quite concretely to mean that

43. MS. Trn. O., inside cover 2. See Herzfeld, p. 32; *Selections*, p. 357.

"Leonardo already sees his 'bird' rising up into the air from the 'Cecero' [Swan], a hill in Florence." And this interpretation is probably correct. But at the same time Leonardo's case offers unique proof that the "technological invention" so characteristic of the West originally sprang from a still unconscious inward reality. Up to the end Leonardo remained a childlike, playful dreamer; everything he did was the symbolic expression of an inward reality. In the last analysis nothing was what it purported to be, or what he himself took it to be. The earnestness of his interest in science, the precision of his work, the technical clarity of his will, and the brilliance of his reasoning in no way alter the fact that—as he himself obscurely felt—everything that he did actually meant something quite different. Only in this way can we explain the continuity of his development, the indefatigable, insatiable course of his life work. And likewise, his desire to fly was in reality more than a technique to be learned, a machine to be built.

How can one prove oneself as a son of the bird mother, of the Great Goddess; what does it mean to "fly" and lift oneself above the earth? These are the symbolically real questions that live in his scientific work.

But Leonardo's flight from the earth, if in this concept we wish to epitomize his rejection of matter, the Earth Mother as lower aspect of the Great Mother, could not, in a nature so vast and so oriented toward wholeness, remain without its inner dialectical countermove. Where the life base is narrower, this constellation of flight from the earth gives rise to delicately lyrical, psychically and intellectually hypersensitive artists, in whom the aesthetic predominates; but with Leonardo's all-encompassing vitality there was bound to be an essential though unconscious countermovement, tending to compensate for his one-sidedness. Herein again he proved to be an authentic son of the Great Mother, who in her wholeness as the Great Round combines the heavenly and the earthly aspect.

Whereas the Middle Ages—and particularly the Gothic period—were dominated by the archetype of the Heavenly Father, the development begun in the Renaissance was based on a revival of the feminine earth archetype. In the course of the last centuries it has led to a revolution of mankind "from below," taking hold of every layer of Western existence. Today the human world as a whole and man as an individual—no longer the celestial world and the nature of the angels—stand at the center of our picture of the world, and man no longer experiences himself as a Lucifer expelled from the celestial paradise, but as an authentic son of the earth. This striking of roots made possible the discovery of the body and natural science, and also of the soul and the unconscious; but underlying all this was the "materialistic" foundation of human existence, which as nature and earth became the foundation of our view of the world as manifested in astronomy and geology, physics and chemistry, biology, sociology, and psychology.[44]

This reversal of the Middle Ages began with the towering figure of Leonardo, who anticipated all these developments, gathered them all in himself, and projected them into the future. But he did not stop here; in

44. Cf. my "Die Bedeutung des Erdarchetyps für die Neuzeit."

the unfolding of his personality he went much farther than the ensuing centuries and our own present age in the integration of all these traits so pregnant with the future.

The generations that came after him developed all the particulars of his world vision; they surpassed him in every field; but they lost what was decisive and most magnificent in Leonardo, namely, the unity. For the essential in Leonardo is not that his mind encompassed such a wide scope of interests, not the encyclopedic aspect of his inquiring will that reached out into the world, but the integration of all this multiplicity into a symbolic human existence. For him nothing had meaning "in itself," nothing was an end in itself, neither the insight nor the practical application, neither the discovery nor the invention, and not even the unity of the opus. For him, almost alone among the artists of the West, art was not everything and not the whole. And also, for him alone among the discoverers and scientists, science was a secret of his individual life, which remained sealed in his copious notebooks, as though it was not important for him to communicate these books, which never became books, to the world.

Unknown to himself, his whole life was directed by the tendency toward an integration of his personality, which experienced itself in the likeness of a godhead encompassing in itself the higher and the lower, heaven and earth. The principle of this unity, which analytical psychology discerned centuries later as the principle of individuation,[45] appears as a mandala, as the Great

45. Cf. the work of Jung on this theme.

Round that—like the Great Goddess—embraces heaven and earth.

Just as his "unearthliness," a medieval trait of his being and his times, was transposed into something entirely new, namely, the scientific problem of flight, so the counterthrust of his nature was also transformed into something revolutionary and charged with future. This counterthrust, as we shall see time and time again in Leonardo, was effected simultaneously on different planes of his being and activity, and this too is a symptom of how totally possessed he was by the processes which were taking place within him and which it required the whole of his many-sided effort to assimilate.[46]

The artistic expression of this situation is a picture unique of its kind, *The Virgin of the Rocks* (Pl. I), of which Merejkowski seems to have given us the profoundest description: "Queen of Heaven, she was shown to men in the gloom of twilight, in a subterranean cavern, in the most secret of the recesses of nature, perhaps the last refuge of ancient Pan and the wood-nymphs—

46. In this essay we shall not arrange Leonardo's biographical data and utterances chronologically, but seek to penetrate the underlying archetypal structure, the pattern. The material of life precipitates in varying depth at the most varying times, so gradually revealing the latent archetypal foundation—as though the inherently rectilinear stream of time was also a circular stream "rotating" above the archetypal structure. For this reason central insights may emerge early in a life and the utterances of the later period need not necessarily be central. Even if a life intention is fulfilled within a definite period, the creative as well as the expressive man does not at all times live at the same stage or at the same depth of his existence.

she the mystery of mysteries, the mother of the God-man, in the very bosom of mother earth." [47]

This madonna is unique. In no other work of art has the secret that light is born of darkness, and that the Spirit Mother of the child savior is one with the sheltering infiniteness of earthly nature, been manifested so eloquently. The triangle, with its base on the earth,[48] which determines the structure of the picture, is an old feminine symbol,[49] the Pythagorean sign of wisdom and space.[50]

The other manifestation of the earth archetype in Leonardo occurs in his scientific work, which in its totality bears witness to this awakening, this Renaissance, which in reality was not a rebirth of antiquity but of the earth. Three areas of his scientific work stand under the sign of the earth, of the Earth Mother: the human body, the earth as an animated organism, and nature as a divine being embracing the two.

Assuredly Leonardo first became interested in anatomy in connection with his work as a painter and sculptor, but how far he advanced beyond this starting point, what vast provinces of nature he discovered in his dissecting of thirty corpses! The drawings and descriptions which

47. Dmitri Merejkowski, *The Romance of Leonardo da Vinci: The Forerunner*, p. 295.

48. Heinrich Wölfflin, *Classic Art*, p. 18.

49. Rudolf Koch, *The Book of Signs*, p. 3.

50. By this remark we do not mean that Leonardo knew this or intentionally smuggled this symbol into the picture. But the agreement of content, structure, and unconscious symbolism nevertheless remains noteworthy.

make up the anatomical study that he planned and largely executed are of such quality that a modern anatomist, writing in 1905, found some of them unequaled even in our times.[51] He made a great number of anatomical discoveries. One writer has gone so far as to declare that "Vesalius's fundamental work on the structure of the human body is nothing but a great plagiarism, a theft from Leonardo's life work." [52] The essential is not that he founded the modern form of topographical anatomy or that he was the first to study comparative anatomy, to establish a correlation between the human organs and those of the animal world. What is most characteristic of his farsightedness and wholeness of outlook is that he was perhaps the first to see anatomy in its functional relationships, so discovering the physiology of the human body. He discovered the great unity of the human circulation, and, as Spengler aptly put it, when he "studied anatomy it was . . . *physiology* studied for the inward secrets"; he "investigated the *life* in the body." [53]

And despite many mistakes in details, what discoveries he made in every field! A hundred years before Kepler he wrote: "The sun does not move," [54] so shaking the

51. Moritz Holl, *Eine Biologe aus der Wende des XV Jahrhundert: Leonardo da Vinci.*

52. Herzfeld, p. cliii.

53. Oswald Spengler, *The Decline of the West,* Vol. I, pp. 277 f.

54. MS. W., fol. 12669ᵛ. See Herzfeld, p. 53; *Selections,* p. 54. J. P. Richter remarks in reference to this passage: "One runs across this passage in the middle of mathematical notes; it is written in uncommonly large letters."

foundations of medieval cosmology. In characterizing this antithesis, Marie Herzfeld quotes the admirable words of Gabriel Séailles: "The stars are incorruptible, divine, without relation to our sublunar world, whose law is generation, change, death. The earth teaches us nothing about the heavens, which belong to a different order. . . . boldly Leonardo shatters this hierarchy; he moves the earth into the heavens." And Leonardo writes: "In your discourse you must prove that the earth is a star much like the moon, and the glory of our universe." [55]

Now it is strange and significant that despite the abundance of Leonardo's fundamental new insights regarding the earth, he should have been held fast by a mythological image of it. He recognized the water cycle and the stratification of the earth caused by sedimentation; he refuted the legend of the Flood and correctly concluded that the fossils lying on the mountains bear witness to the existence of oceans that once covered these mountains. But the passion that he devoted to his investigations, his fascination with their object, the earth, led him to animate it. How alive this earth-body equation was for him may be seen from the following quotation:

"The water which rises in the mountains is the blood which keeps the mountain in life. If one of its veins be open either internally or at the side, nature, which assists its organisms, abounding in increased desire to over-

55. MS. F., fol. 56ʳ. See Herzfeld, p. 59; *Selections*, p. 54.

come the scarcity of moisture thus poured out, is prodigal there in indulgent aid, as also happens with the place at which a man has received a blow. For one sees then how as help comes the blood increases under the skin in the form of a swelling in order to open the infected part. Similarly, life being severed at the topmost extremity (of the mountain), nature sends her fluid from its lowest foundations up to the greatest height of the severed passage, and as this is poured out there it does not leave it bereft of vital fluid down to the end of its life." [56]

And in botany he finds the same law of compensation, for Mother Nature never leaves her creatures "bereft": "When a tree has had part of its bark stripped off, nature in order to provide for it supplies to the stripped portion a far greater quantity of nutritive moisture than to any other part; so that, because of the first scarcity which has been referred to, the bark there grows much more thickly than in any other place." [57]

This maternal character of the earth is so much a certainty to him that he experiences the earth in the image of a living body: [58] "So then we may say that the earth

56. MS. H., fol. 77ʳ. See Herzfeld, p. 63; MacCurdy, Vol. I, p. 77.

57. MS. C.A., fol. 76ʳ. See Herzfeld, p. 120; MacCurdy, Vol. I, p. 317.

58. One of his riddles runs as follows: "Many there will be who will flay their own mother and fold back her skin." The answer is: "The tillers of the ground." (MS. I., fol. 64ʳ. See Herzfeld p. 279; *Selections*, p. 245.) The archetypal character of this formulation is shown by the flaying which played so prominent a part in the fertility rites of ancient Mexico.

has a spirit of growth; that its flesh is the soil; its bones are the successive strata of the rocks which form the mountains, its muscles are the tufastone, its blood the springs of its water. The lake of blood that lies about the heart is the ocean. . . . " [59]

Nature is the Great Goddess herself; she bestows on the maternal earth as upon the human mother the vegetative soul that "nourishes and animates the child."

"Nature places the soul in said body, the formative soul, namely, the soul of the mother, who first forms in her womb the shape of man and at a fitting time awakens the soul which is to be its inhabitant, which was formerly dormant and in the safeguard of the mother's soul, which she nourishes and animates through the navel cord with all her spiritual organs, and will so continue as long as this navel is connected with the fruit and the seed leaves, whereby the child is joined with the mother." [60]

It was said of Leonardo: "In nature he finds time and time again something to learn; he is devoted to her as a son to his mother." [61] And this is true in a far deeper and more fundamental sense than this "poetic image" might at first lead us to suppose.

Here it is not our task to discuss Leonardo's importance as a scientist, which lies most of all in his discovery of scientific experiment. "Experience does not err," he

59. R. 1000, MS. Leic., fol. 34ʳ. See Herzfeld, p. 62; MacCurdy, Vol. I, p. 91.
60. R. 837, MS. W. AN. IV, fol. 184ʳ. See Herzfeld, p. 119.
61. Herzfeld, p. 119.

wrote; "it is only your judgment that errs in expecting from her what is not in her power." [62]

What concerns us is how very much alive the archetype of the Great Mother, the unity of the heaven-and-earth goddess, was in Leonardo's life and work. She lived for him not only as a mythological image, but in his scientific work was raised to the level of a scientific view of the world.

Thus he speaks of the "ever generative goddess": "Nature is full of infinite causes that have never occurred in experience." [63]

Or: "The genius of man may make various inventions, encompassing with various instruments one and the same end; but it will never discover a more beautiful, a more economical, or a more direct one than nature's, since in her inventions nothing is wanting and nothing is superfluous." [64]

But he did not succumb to a romantic transfiguration of nature. Side by side with the Good Mother he also recognized the Terrible Mother in her, as follows clearly from a sentence whose insight and perspective seem so characteristic of Leonardo: "Here nature appears to have been a cruel stepmother to many animals instead of a mother, and to some not a stepmother but a most tender mother." [65]

His evaluation is no longer Christian and medieval.

62. MS. C.A., fol. 154ʳ. See Herzfeld, p. 5; *Selections,* p. 5.

63. MS. I., fol. 18ʳ. See Herzfeld, p. 11; *Selections,* p. 7.

64. MS. W., fol. 19116ʳ. See Herzfeld, pp. 118–19; *Selections,* p. 103.

65. MS. S.K.M. III, fol. 20ᵛ. See Herzfeld, p. 117; *Selections,* p. 278.

He sees that "Our life is made by the death of others," [66] but this does not fill him with a sense of guilt; it does not prove to him the fallen state of man, darkened by original sin. This earth too is a star, and man, potentially at least, is a divine creator, although he belongs to the animal world.

"In fact, man does not vary from the animals except in what is accidental, and it is in this that he shows himself to be a divine thing; for where nature finishes producing its species, there man begins with natural things to make with the aid of this nature an infinite number of species; and as these are not necessary to those who govern themselves rightly as do the animals, it is not in their disposition to seek after them." [67]

And: "The painter strives and competes with nature." [68]

But in this rivalry and this "godlikeness," Leonardo is not Luciferian; he is humbly devoted to nature and the earth. In contrast to the decree of the Heavenly Spirit of the Scholastics, which determined all life deductively "from above," the modern man in Leonardo bowed down to the earth.

"All our knowledge," he wrote, "has its origin in our perceptions." [69] Here "perceptions" might be translated as "actual experience," for "Where there is the most

66. MS. H., fol. 89ᵛ. See Herzfeld, p. 117; *Selections*, p. 278.
67. Sp. MS. W. AN. B., fol. 13ʳ. See Herzfeld, 4th ed., pp. 104–5; MacCurdy, Vol. I, p. 129.
68. MS. S.K.M. III, fol. 44ᵛ. See Herzfeld, p. 159; *Selections*, p. 216.
69. MS. Triv., fol. 20ᵛ. See Herzfeld, p. 131; *Selections*, p. 4.

sensation, there is the greatest martyrdom," [70] i.e., pain and suffering.[71]

But with all his awareness of his divine creative power, Leonardo, son of maternal nature, remains a "servant" in his humble devotion to the earth. "I am never weary of serving." [72] "Obstacles do not bend me." "Every obstacle yields to firm resolve." [73]

"No labor is sufficient to tire me," he writes, and continues: "Hands into which ducats and precious stones fall like snow; they never become tired of serving, but this service is only for its utility and not according to our intention." And he concludes with the proud words: "Naturally nature has so disposed me." [74]

This sense of service draws its unshakable power from the intense alertness of a higher being. It is the alertness of consciousness that here appears as activity and movement, as the psychic core of the human and the creative: "Rather death than weariness!"

"O thou that sleepest, what is sleep?" writes Leonardo. "Sleep resembles death; oh, why not let thy work be such that after death thou mayst retain a resemblance to

70. MS. Triv., fol. 6. See Herzfeld, p. 131.

71. That Leonardo's remark about sensation has nothing to do with a materialistic theory of knowledge may be shown by his aphorism: "The senses are of the earth; the reason stands apart from them in contemplation." (MS. Triv., fol. 33ʳ. See Herzfeld, p. 131; *Selections*, p. 6.)

72. R. 685, MS. W.P., fol. 11ᵛ. See Herzfeld, p. 139.

73. R. 682, MS. W.L., fol. 198ʳ. See Herzfeld, p. 141; J. P. Richter (ed.), *The Literary Works of Leonardo da Vinci*, Vol. I, p. 382, No. 682.

74. R. 685, MS. W.P., fol. 11ᵛ. Cf. Herzfeld, p. 139; cf. Richter, *Literary Works*, Vol. I, p. 389, No. 685.

perfect life, rather than during life make thyself resemble the hapless dead by sleeping." [75]

The work he intended is no finished work like the work of the artist or scientist, however great; his intention is manifested in the symbol of "alertness," of "not-being-tired."

"Intellectual passion drives out sensuality," [76] he writes. This highly characteristic utterance proves that with him it was a question not only of repressing and inhibiting the world of the drives, and not only of sublimating energies to a higher plane, but of a regrouping in which a genuine power, which Leonardo designates as the "passion of the spirit," becomes dominant. For the spirit too is a genuine "driving force" of the human psyche.

The hero-son in the myth is not only the son of the Virgin Mother but also of the Spirit Father who fecundates her. This "mythological situation," which in Leonardo—as in all creative men—takes the form of the search for the "true father," the Spirit Father, leads as a rule to two complementary events: the "slaying of the collective father," i.e., the surpassing of the traditional value world of the hero's time; and the finding of the unknown God.

In Leonardo the slaying of the father is evinced in his radically antiauthoritarian, antischolastic, and anticonfessional attitude, which was so strong that the men of his time thought him "suspect" and even—though

75. MS. C.A., fol. 76ᵛ. See Herzfeld, p. 122; *Selections,* p. 274.
76. MS. C.A., fol. 358ᵛ. See Herzfeld, p. 140; MacCurdy, Vol. I, p. 72.

mistakenly—anti-Christian. "Whoever in discussion adduces authority uses not intellect but rather memory," [77] he wrote. The full import of these words can be understood only if we consider not only that the science and medicine of his time were built on the authority of the ancients, but that the entire religious edifice of the Middle Ages was also founded on the "authority" of the Bible and its exegetes. With this protest, to be sure, Leonardo followed an inner call that often made itself heard at that time, but his dangerous proximity to heresy was assuredly one of his reasons for putting down his notes in mirror writing and only as a record for his own use. This danger is obvious when we consider Spengler's sentence: "When Leonardo da Vinci, at the summit of the Renaissance, was working upon his 'Anna Selbdritt,' the Witches' Hammer was being written in Rome in the finest humanistic Latin." [78]

A part of his heretical attitudes and thoughts is hidden in his riddles. One of them runs: "In all parts of Europe there shall be lamentations by great nations for the death of one man who died in the East." [79] And the solution is: "The lamentations made on Good Friday." Or—and this was before the Reformation—his riddle on the worship of images of saints: "Men shall speak with men who hear not; their eyes shall be open and they

77. MS. C.A., fol. 76ʳ. See Herzfeld, p. 9; MacCurdy, Vol. I, p. 95.
78. Spengler, Vol. II, pp. 291–92. [Anna Selbdritt = St. Anne, Virgin, and Christ Child, as an art motif. Witches' Hammer = *Malleus Maleficarum*, manual on the punishment of witches.— Ed.]
79. MS. C.A., fol. 370ʳ. See Herzfeld, p. 297; *Selections*, p. 248.

shall not see: they will speak to them and there shall be no reply; they will ask pardon from one who has ears and does not hear; they will offer light to one who is blind." [80]

These are iconoclastic words, especially in the mouth of a painter of madonnas and saints. They are no less revolutionary than the riddle "of churches and the habitations of friars": "Many there will be who will give up work and labor, and poverty of life and of goods, and will go to live among wealth in splendid buildings, declaring that this is the way to make themselves acceptable to God." [81]

The antiauthoritarian attitude of the hero, whose mission it is to usher in the new, is archetypally conditioned and cannot, as Freud attempts to do, be derived from Leonardo's childhood history—a history falsely construed to begin with. Freud writes: "In most other human beings—no less today than in primeval times—the need for support from an authority of some sort is so compelling that their world begins to totter if that authority is threatened. Only Leonardo could dispense with that support; he would not have been able to do so had he not learnt in the first years of his life to do without his father." [82]

As so often in Freud, what is false when considered on the personalistic plane is true on the archetypal plane. The hero's Spirit Father, his inner "pneumatic" reality, the "wind" that fecundates the vulture goddess,

80. MS. C.A., fol. 137ʳ. See Herzfeld, p. 292; *Selections,* p. 249.
81. MS. C.A., fol. 370ᵛ. See Herzfeld, p. 302; *Selections,* p. 249.
82. Freud, pp. 122–23.

is unknown to the hero. He experiences "everything" through the mother, who as "Great Mother" also contains within her the masculine and the spiritual aspects. We also find this constellation in the normal development of the child—in the Western world at least. Only gradually does the child free himself from the uroboric Great Mother of the original relation, whose one world then separates into oppositions dominated by the mother and father archetype, and finally turns into the patriarchal world dominated by the father archetype. But in the "hero" the constellation is different. Estrangement from his personal father and the world he represents then leads the hero to the "quest" for his "real father," the spiritual authority, from which he is essentially descended.

But whereas the heroes who are "Father's sons" attain to an experience of unity in the dragon fight ("I and the Father are one"), the "Mother's sons," even if they have found their relation to the Spirit Father, always remain closer to the Mother, in whom the supreme godhead is manifested to them. In this case it is not infrequent for the paternal-male principle to be juxtaposed or subordinated to the maternal principle, as is the rule in the matriarchal phase.

Thus in Leonardo's religious experience the paternal spirit-godhead as the newly discovered unknown God remained subordinated to the Mother Goddess—although Leonardo was not conscious of this. As demiurge, as master builder, inventor, and constructor, Leonardo praised the creative God, and his religious feeling rises up time and time again from the fervent emotion inspired in him by his knowledge of nature and its laws.

"How admirable thy justice, O thou First Mover!" he cried out. "Thou hast not willed that any power should be deprived of the processes or qualities necessary for its results." [83] This formulation still bears the stamp of the Platonizing philosophy of his time. But as his formulations became more closely integrated with his own researches, his imagery became richer and more concrete. "Let no man who is not a mathematician read the fundamentals of my work." [84] This sentence may be said to anticipate the development of the natural sciences, yet it is not Leonardo's profoundest insight.

"Necessity is the mistress and guide of nature.

"Necessity is the theme and inventor of nature, its eternal curb and law." [85]

"Nature does not break her law." [86]

The bond between the Spirit Father as law, as fundamental idea or reason, and the Great Goddess Nature is the archetypal foundation of all pantheistic conceptions. Mythologically, the wind fecundates the vulture goddess and engenders movement in her; it is the spirit law of her vitality. At the corresponding stage of insight Leonardo declares: "Nature is constrained by the logical necessity of her law, which is infused in her." [87] And the mythological image of the spirit seed is still discernible in the image of the "infusing."

83. MS. A., fol. 24ʳ. See Herzfeld, p. 22; *Selections*, p. 76.

84. MS. W., fol. 19118ᵛ. See Herzfeld, p. 3; *Selections*, p. 7.

85. MS. S.K.M. III, fol. 43ʳ. See Herzfeld, p. 12; *Selections*, p. 7.

86. MS. C., fol. 23ᵛ. See Herzfeld, p. 12; *Selections*, p. 7.

87. MS. C., fol. 23ᵛ. See Herzfeld, p. 12; *Selections*, p. 7 (mod.).

Here we find a strange similarity between Leonardo and Spinoza, who was in other ways so very different from him. I am referring not only to the "mathematical method" foreshadowed by Leonardo and to the "deus sive natura" that for Spinoza as well was no materialistic conception, but most particularly to the principle of "love out of knowledge," which for both men was the highest form of human realization. Leonardo said: "For painting is the way to learn to know the maker of all marvelous things, and this is the way to love so great an inventor. For in truth love springs from the full knowledge of the thing that one loves; and if you do not know it, you can love it but little or not at all." [88]

And like an echo Spinoza answers, almost 150 years later: "This kind of knowledge . . . result[s] . . . from a direct revelation of the object itself to the understanding. And if that object is glorious and good, then the soul becomes necessarily united with it. . . . Hence it follows incontrovertibly that it is this knowledge which evokes love." [89]

This "gnostic" attitude of love through knowledge [90] under the auspices of the Spirit Father contrasts with the unconscious feeling tone of his relation to the Great

88. From the *Traktat von der Malerei* [*Trattato della Pittura*], p. 54; *Selections*, p. 217.

89. A. Wolf (tr.), *Spinoza's Short Treatise on God, Man, and his Well-Being*, Part II, ch. 22, p. 133.

90. The transition to Spinoza is supplied by the Renaissance philosophy of love, whose most significant exponent was Leo Hebraeus. His *Dialoghi d'amore* appeared in 1535.

Mother, discernible in his words of proud gratitude: "Naturally nature has so disposed me."

His bond with nature is direct and primary, his love of knowledge derived and secondary, just as the mother is direct and first for the child, the father derived and second.

Only when we grasp these inner developments and experiences in Leonardo can we conceive of the loneliness in which he lived. The situation of the hero-son who experiences himself as son of a Spirit Father unknown in his contemporary world is always that of gnostic "existence in an alien world." But in Leonardo this one-sided gnostic constellation is compensated and complicated by the "Mother's son's" earthliness and profound affirmation of life. This central conflict explains the ambiguity and splitness of his existence. He, the illegitimate child, moved among the aristocracy, the princes, kings, and popes of his time, with the lonely aristocracy of genius, which though admired from afar is understood and loved by no one.

Leonardo saw in man the great and perfect work of nature; in a marginal note to some anatomical drawings and expositions he wrote: "And thou, man, who in this work of mine dost look upon the wonderful works of nature, if thou judgest it to be a criminal thing to destroy it, reflect how much more criminal it is to take the life of man; and if this external form appears to thee marvelously constructed, remember that it is as nothing compared with the soul that dwells in that structure; and in truth, whatever this may be, it is a thing divine. Leave it then to dwell in its work at its good pleasure, and let not thy rage and malice destroy such a life—for in truth he who values it not does not deserve it." [91]

But this same respect for man fills him with loveless contempt for the rabble, which is not creative and therefore not made in the divine image: "It seems to me that coarse men of bad habits and little power of reason do not deserve so fine an instrument or so great a variety of mechanism as those endowed with ideas and great reasoning power, but merely a sack where food is received and whence it passes. For in truth they cannot be reckoned otherwise than as a passage for food, because it does not seem to me that they have anything in common with the human race except voice and shape. And all else is far below the level of beasts." [92]

The same Leonardo who was opposed to the taking of life, who was a vegetarian,[93] and who was said, even in the days of his poverty, to have bought birds in the market only to set them free—this same Leonardo dissected live frogs, constructed the most frightful war machines, and even boasted of being their inventor. He was an intimate adviser of Cesare Borgia; he studied the physiognomy and made sketches of men on their way to be executed. This unique painter of the soul's beauty was without equal in his discernment of the bestial and evil in the human face; he was the first to see man as an ape, as a caricature of himself.

91. MS. W., fol. 19001ʳ. See Herzfeld, p. 137; *Selections,* p. 280.
92. MS. W., fol. 19038. See Herzfeld, p. 105; *Selections,* p. 279.
93. R. Langton Douglas, *Leonardo da Vinci: His Life and His Pictures,* p. 1.

Leonardo suffered from this tension between the contraries of heaven and earth; in his realm beyond good and evil he was as lonely as scarcely another creative man before Nietzsche. For he had no ties with even the greatest among his contemporaries. He was as alien to Michelangelo's titanic preoccupation with his opus as to Raphael's unquestioning felicity. The "unreliable," problematic Leonardo who never finished anything lived as an outsider and almost as an outcast among the famous men of his time. And yet with all his many-sidedness, and despite his desperate inability to fulfill himself in any one thing, Leonardo was never restless, never hunted. He was anything but a "problematic nature" in the usual sense, let alone a sick man "incapable" of doing his work.

The task he set himself—of combining in art the law and necessity of the spirit, which he sought to apprehend in the measurements and proportions of the body, with the creative spontaneity of nature's beauty—was so immense and paradoxical that the product was almost bound to be experimental and fragmentary. Equally paradoxical was his striving to build a higher unity from infinite space and the open, unconfined human form, from depth of background and fullness of foreground, and from the opposition between light and shade in all its transitions and gradations. "Leonardo begins with the inside, the spiritual space within us, not with the considered definition-line, and when he ends . . . the substance of color lies like a mere breathing over the real structure of the picture." [94]

94. Spengler, Vol. I, pp. 277–78.

Here again the aim is a synthesis of spirit and nature, of the infinite and finite, of the invisible reality of a soul grown visible and the tangible reality of a body unlimited in space. Leonardo was captivated by the paradoxical character of these problems and devoted to them with the entire passion of his nature; yet at the same time he saw them from a distance, just as he saw himself from outside. This is most clearly revealed by the strange form of his notes; he never writes "I will," "I should," but, as though a strange voice were speaking to him, "You must," "you should." This distance, this tireless attempt, never abandoned in all the passion of his work, to achieve a midpoint between the contraries which he experienced and suffered in all their depth and power is indeed the unique in Leonardo.

He was open to everything; he was the son of the Mother as well as the Father. He suffered within himself a crossing of the vertical—Spirit, medieval man, and the heavenly Father—with the horizontal—earth-bound and earth-oriented modern man and the Great Mother. It was in this crossing of heaven and earth, which is the Cross of the modern man,[95] that Leonardo discovered man's new position between the powers.

His *Last Supper,* it seems to me, is an expression of this struggle and of this synthesis of opposites. In the Christ of this painting the synthesis of God and man, of above and below, is perceived and configured in an entirely new way. This Son of Man surrounded by the disciples is an archetypal yet real and earthly, that is, incarnate, image of primordial man. He is the image of

95. Jung, *Aion,* index, s.v.

what man "really and essentially" is. Leonardo's Christ is no sufferer, no man of pain, nor is he the Christ of the Gospel of St. John. He is more human, for he is the very core of the human, around which the disciples representing the different temperaments that make up human nature are dramatically yet harmoniously grouped. He is not only the "man from the East" and the man who stands alone; he is not only the youthful God incarnate; he is the transfiguration of all that is human, the loneliness of the wise. And in his outspread arms there lives the receptive silence of him who surrenders to the necessity of a destiny which is his very own self.

We know how long and perseveringly—with a perseverance characteristic of him despite his fragmentary work—Leonardo struggled with this painting. If he left the face of Christ unfinished, this only proves that he remained faithful to his inner image, and was not concerned with the ideal of completeness that means so much to mankind and was so particularly important to his time. This image of man, which first manifested itself to Leonardo, had to remain incomplete; for incompleteness is intrinsic in the human and earthly, as Leonardo, perhaps the first of modern men, experienced it in the suffering of his own existence.

But the struggle with the Great Mother, the central theme of Leonardo's life, was never appeased; it led him, at the age of fifty, to the supreme and ultimate creations, not only of European painting, but of all creative embodiment of the feminine.

The *Mona Lisa* and the *St. Anne with Virgin and Christ Child* are the incomparable expressions of this period, in which the feminine through Leonardo was manifested to the Western world in a new and, in a sense, definitive form. It is no accident that the *Mona Lisa* has fascinated innumerable thousands of men for centuries or that this painting occupies a unique place in European painting. But why does the *Mona Lisa,* of all the European portraits of women, pass as the embodiment of the riddle of the feminine; why does this smile time and time again invite interpretation, as though confronting modern man with a question that calls for an answer?

In this painting the feminine appears in a unique way, not as Heavenly Goddess or Earth Mother, but as a human soul in which the heavenly and the earthly achieve a new synthesis. There is in Mona Lisa something ambiguous and indefinable, something fugitive and mystical, a fascination and a mysterious sensuality; but one might say equally well that all this is manifested through her. For in the endlessness of the background, in the color transitions, the merging of light and shade, there lives a soul which is embodied equally in Mona Lisa herself and in the landscape, in the indescribable unity of the picture and in every one of its details, the hands, the smile, the mountains of the background, or the serpentine leading to the mystery of the blue lakes.

"The presence that rose thus so strangely beside the waters, is expressive of what in the ways of a thousand years men had come to desire. Hers is the head upon which all 'the ends of the world are come,' and the eyelids are a little weary. It is a beauty wrought out from within upon the flesh, the deposit, little cell by cell, of

strange thoughts and fantastic reveries and exquisite passions. Set it for a moment beside one of those white
Greek goddesses or beautiful women of antiquity, and
how would they be troubled by this beauty, into which
the soul with all its maladies has passed! All the thoughts
and experience of the world have etched and molded
there, in that which they have of power to refine and
make expressive the outward form, the animalism of
Greece, the lust of Rome, the mysticism of the middle
age with its spiritual ambition and imaginative loves,
the return of the Pagan world, the sins of the Borgias.
She is older than the rocks among which she sits; like
the vampire, she has been dead many times, and learned
the secrets of the grave; and has been a diver in deep
seas, and keeps their fallen day about her; and trafficked
for strange webs with Eastern merchants; and as Leda,
was the mother of Helen of Troy, and, as St. Anne, the
mother of Mary; and all this has been to her but as the
sound of lyres and flutes, and lives only in the delicacy
with which it has molded the changing lineaments, and
tinged the eyelids and the hands. The fancy of a perpetual life, sweeping together ten thousand experiences,
is an old one; and modern philosophy has conceived the
idea of humanity as wrought upon by, and summing up
in itself, all modes of thought and life. Certainly Lady
Lisa might stand as the embodiment of the old fancy,
the symbol of the modern idea." [96]

The mediating and indefinable, the gentle and cruel,
the far and near, actual and yet timeless, which Pater

96. Walter Pater, *The Renaissance; Studies in Art and Poetry,*
pp. 129–30.

expressed in this almost magical picture, correspond almost exactly to the archetypal soul image of the feminine, the anima, later discovered by depth psychology. And it is extremely significant that only Leonardo, who had freed himself from the reality of all earthly bonds, should have succeeded in conjuring up this figure of the feminine soul. In Mona Lisa the immortal beloved appeared to this man of fifty as Sophia, as man's intangible and transcendent counterpart.

In Valentinian Gnosis, "the world soul was born of Sophia's smile." [97] And with Mona Lisa's smile was born the soul of modern man, in which Madonna and witch, the earthly, and the divine, are combined.[98]

The break-through that occurred in Leonardo's encounter with Mona Lisa led in his life to the victory of Eros over Logos, of love over knowledge. The words "Love conquers everything," [99] which would sound banal on any other lips, seem in Leonardo, for whom love was born from knowledge, to express a new insight.

All of Leonardo's great paintings after *Mona Lisa* must be understood in the light of this Eros, which transformed and renewed his life. This is most evident in connection with the *St. Anne* (Pl. II), in which he

97. G. Quispel, *Gnosis als Weltreligion*, n. 76.

98. This picture, on which Leonardo worked for four years, also remained unfinished. Mona Lisa died suddenly at the age of twenty-six. Leonardo, who kept this picture with him to the end of his life, may himself have perceived the bond between life and death that lies like a veil of unreality on her mysterious face.

99. MS. C.A., fol. 344ʳ. See Herzfeld, p. 149; MacCurdy, Vol. I, p. 96.

achieved a magnificent new conception of the Holy Mothers.

In addition to the unity of mother and daughter, Demeter and Kore, the matriarchal group in Eleusis includes a third: the divine daughter or the divine son.[100] In the Christian paintings of *St. Anne with Virgin and Christ Child* this primordial matriarchal figure enters into a predominantly patriarchal-Christian realm. For this reason Mary, holding the child Jesus, is often represented as herself a child sitting in her mother's lap. St. Anne thus appears as the all-embracing fountainhead of the generations, as a form of "Great Mother" living on in Christianity.[101]

According to her legend, St. Anne belongs to the archetypal group of women who, barren with their earthly husbands, are impregnated by the godhead. Later, this mythological impregnation by the god is usually replaced by the god's promise to the barren woman. According to the legend, St. Anne married three husbands, gave birth to innumerable saints, and is the patron saint of childbirth and mines; all this bears witness to her original fertility aspect as Earth Mother. In Christian painting she wears over a red undergarment, the symbol of love, the green mantle of nature in contrast to the blue mantle of Mary, who represents the Sophia-Spirit aspect.

In Masaccio's work the figure of St. Anne fills the

100. C. Kerényi, "Kore," pp. 198 ff. in *Essays on a Science of Mythology*, cf. my *Great Mother*, pp. 305 f.

101. We owe this discovery to Olga Froebe-Kapteyn, founder of the Eranos Archive in Ascona, Switzerland.

background; in a protective attitude reminiscent of the mantle madonnas, she still enfolds Mary and the Child in her outspread arms.

In the symbolic figures of Anne and Mary we discern the contrast between the "elementary" and "transformative" character of the Archetypal Feminine.[102] To simplify, the elementary character corresponds to the maternal, containing, childbearing, nurturing, and protective aspect; while the transformative character, in its highest form, corresponds to the Sophia aspect of the feminine.

The historical circumstances surrounding the painting of Leonardo's picture are not without interest. The *St. Anne* was ordered in 1500 by the Servites for the Church of the Santissima Annunziata in Florence.

"During that period, the religious orders that were devoted to the cult of Mary had stressed the importance of the doctrine of the Immaculate Conception. The acceptance of this dogma led, in the course of time, to the adoption of the thesis that the Virgin's mother was a woman of great sanctity. The old legends relating that St. Anne had three husbands and three daughters became more and more discredited. This movement in Catholic theology reached its culminating point in 1494, on the publication of a book in praise of St. Anne, by a famous German scholar, Johannes Trithemius, Abbot of Sponheim.[103] St. Anne, wrote the author, was chosen by God for her appointed service before the foundation of the world. She conceived 'without the action of man,'

102. Cf. my *Great Mother*, pp. 24 f.
103. Johannes Trithemius, *De laudibus Sanctissimae Matris Annae tractatus* (1494).

and was as pure as her daughter. 'Why then,' Trithemius asks, 'do we not honor the mother as we honor
the daughter?'" [104]

This doctrine of St. Anne's virginity, later rejected by
the Church, gave Leonardo the opportunity to awaken
the archetypal image of the feminine that lay dormant in
his unconscious and to represent the mother-daughter
archetype in the unity of Anne and Mary.

At first sight Leonardo's picture seems to retain the
usual pattern. St. Anne's silhouette enfolds Mary, who is
sitting on her lap; the two form a unit. In Leonardo's
(differently composed) cartoon for *St. Anne* (Pl. III),
one is almost tempted to speak of a two-headed figure.
This condensation of the "two mothers" into one figure,
noted by Freud,[105] springs from an archetypal constellation characterized by the myth in which the hero possesses an earthly and a heavenly mother.[106]

However, St. Anne is usually represented as mother
and Mary as daughter. But Leonardo's figures are eternally youthful twin figures of the feminine. They too,
like the Eleusinian Demeter and Kore, might be called
"the goddesses." [107] But in Leonardo there is a strange reversal. Mary, as she bends forward to clasp the child,
represents the maternal, elementary character of the
feminine; the smiling St. Anne dwells in the spiritual,
transformative realm of Sophia,[108] which here forms a

104. Douglas, p. 26.
105. *Leonardo*, pp. 111 ff.
106. Often, though not always, the opposition of good and evil
is involved.
107. Cf. my *Great Mother*, pp. 305 f.
108. Cf. ibid., pp. 329 f.

background even more meaningful and mysterious than in the *Mona Lisa.*

This reversal, in which the Sophia-Spirit-transformative character outweighs the elementary character of the maternal, is the symbolic expression of an archetypal situation that seems to be characteristic not only for Leonardo but for modern man in general.

Where the elementary character of the feminine is predominant, as in matriarchally accented epochs, the psychic world is relatively static, for the rule of the Great Mother implies not only a domination of the unconscious over consciousness [109] but also a relatively stable situation. Such cultures are conservative and even in a certain sense reactionary, because the instinctual aspect of the unconscious, represented by the archetype of the Great Mother, dictates a fixed system of unconscious attitudes, in which there is little room for the initiative and activity of the ego and consciousness, that is, of the masculine aspect. In opposition to a situation in which the Great Mother dominates her son-lover, the hero, with his development of the ego and consciousness, represents a "fresh attempt" on the part of the psyche. But where the elementary character of the feminine predominates, the masculine youth—to formulate it mythologically—is the "thing of a season." He is condemned to an early death; the unconscious assimilates all the activities of the ego, employing them for its own purposes, and prevents it from ripening to the reality of an independent world of consciousness.

Medieval man was "contained" in the bosom of

109. See my *Origins and History,* pp. 40 f.

Mother Church. But when the transformative became predominant over the elementary character, this meant that henceforth the transformation of consciousness and of the total personality would be the theme of Western development.

The synchronistic growth of alchemical literature, which, as Jung has shown,[110] was an attempt to express this process of psychic transformation, and many other "signs of the times," such as the Reformation, indicate that the center of psychic life was beginning to shift to the individual. The Renaissance has justly been called the epoch of the discovery of the individual. In the following centuries the individual and his destiny, the problem of his containment in the collective psyche—in the collectivity without and within—come increasingly to the forefront in politics, art, literature, sociology, and psychology.

The indefatigable mobility which prevented Leonardo from stopping at any work or insight and drove him to change continuously is an expression of this unrest in modern man, who was beginning to take cognizance of the endlessness and mystery of the psyche. It was no accident that Walter Pater should have discovered this transformative character precisely in Leonardo's feminine figures, in the *Mona Lisa* and the women of the Holy Family, of whom he says:

". . . They are the clairvoyants, through whom, as through delicate instruments, one becomes aware of the subtler forces of nature, and the modes of their action, all that is magnetic in it, all those finer conditions

110. Especially in *Psychology and Alchemy*.

wherein material things rise to that subtlety of operation which constitutes them spiritual, where only the finer nerve and the keener touch can follow. It is as if in certain significant examples we actually saw those forces at their work on human flesh. Nervous, electric, faint always with some inexplicable faintness, these people seem to be subject to exceptional conditions, to feel powers at work in the common air unfelt by others, to become, as it were, the receptacle of them, and pass them on to us in a chain of secret influences." [111]

In Leonardo's painting the daughter who gives birth to the savior represents, then, the elementary character; she is subordinated to St. Anne as the Great Mother and source of spiritual transformation. And here we find manifested an archetypal constellation whose revolutionary import we cannot fully fathom even today.

After Leonardo, Goethe alone of Western men disclosed the same tendency toward individuation in an infinitely mobile unity of life and work. It is no mistake to regard Leonardo as a "Faustian man." In Goethe's *Faust* the archetypal constellations to which Leonardo gave form achieve conscious formulation. And what Goethe says of the Mothers is fully in keeping with their transformative character: "Formation, transformation, eternal preservation of the eternal meaning."

And the constellation of the *St. Anne* also reappears at the end of Part II of *Faust*. To the double form of Anne-Mary raising the son aloft corresponds the Eternal Feminine, drawing the child Faust "onward." The vulture goddess is the Goddess of Heaven. In Leonardo's paint-

111. Pater, p. 120.

ing St. Anne's head towers into the ethereal world of
heaven. And in Goethe:

> Höchste Herrscherin der Welt
> Lasse mich im blauen
> Ausgespannten Himmelszelt
> Dein Geheimnis schauen.

> (Supreme goddess of the world
> Let me behold thy secret
> In the blue unfolded
> Tent of heaven.)

Strangely enough, the unity of the matriarchal group
of Anne, Mary, and the Child with the vulture, the

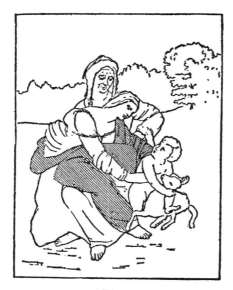

Fig. 1

archetypal symbol of the Great Mother, is expressed, though obscurely, in Leonardo's painting. The discovery was made by Pfister (cf. Fig. 1): "In the length of blue cloth, which is visible around the hip of the woman in front and which extends in the direction of her lap and her right knee, one can see the vulture's extremely characteristic head, its neck and the sharp curve where its body begins. Hardly any observer whom I have confronted with my little find has been able to resist the evidence of this picture-puzzle." [112]

Quite naturally, Freud and Pfister connect the unconscious image of the vulture with Leonardo's childhood recollection. In the picture the vulture's tail, as in the fantasy, is over the mouth of the child, who turns his head upward while holding the little lamb at his feet.

The question now arises as to whether Freud's "mistake," which we have discussed at some length above, discredits Pfister's discovery. For if the bird in Leonardo's childhood reminiscence was not a vulture but a *nibio,* a kite, why should the form of a vulture turn up in the *St. Anne with Virgin and Christ Child?* Strachey's answer is that "the 'hidden bird' in Leonardo's picture must be abandoned." [113] But if we look into the matter more deeply, we shall come to a different conclusion. Pfister and Freud had in mind an *unconscious* figure, and there is no reason to suppose that such an unconscious image must coincide with Leonardo's conscious reminiscence of the "kite." If with Pfister and Freud we

112. O. Pfister, "Kryptolalie, Kryptographie und unbewusstes Vexierbild bei Normalen," p. 147. (Tr. as in Freud, p. 115.)
113. Strachey, editorial note to Freud, p. 61.

recognize—and so we do—the form of a vulture touching the Christ Child's lips with its tail, our picture-puzzle is just as much in need of interpretation as before—more so in fact, for now we must ask: how did the conscious recollection of a kite become transformed into the unconscious image of a vulture? But in formulating this question we have almost answered it. The conscious recollection of the zoologically definable kite has been replaced by the symbolic image characteristic of the Great Mother. Regardless of whether we suppose this form to have sprung from an archetypal image—and we know that such images can arise spontaneously in men possessing no "knowledge" of them—or whether we assume that Leonardo was aware of the mother-significance of the vulture, Freud supports his assumption that Leonardo, who was very widely read, knew of the vulture as a mother symbol by pointing out that the Church Fathers, in speaking of the virgin birth, repeatedly cited the legend of the female vulture fertilized by the wind. This "vulture image" occurs in a picture of St. Anne, who as we have seen is closely connected with the problem of "virgin birth." Having noted this connection, we can scarcely help wondering whether the "hidden vulture," far from being a product of the unconscious, might not have been consciously put into the picture by Leonardo. This seems perfectly compatible with his playful nature and love of mystery. But in any case, whether we believe that the vulture found its way consciously or unconsciously into the picture of St. Anne, the fact remains that its tail touches the child's mouth as in his childhood reminiscence. In other words, Leonardo related this fundamental constellation of the "divine child" with the "divine mother" to himself, and identified himself with this child. If our basic assumption that Leonardo's whole work was a self-unfolding of his individuation process is correct, there is nothing surprising about this phenomenon. But in any event—and this must be emphasized here—if the picture-puzzle is unconscious rather than conscious, Freud's "mistake" corresponds to a mistake by Leonardo himself. In both men the symbolic image of the Great Mother proved stronger than the actual image of the "kite."

If we follow the right edge of the large triangle into which Leonardo, as in *The Virgin of the Rocks,* composed the figures of this picture, we obtain an ascending sequence of symbolic figures embracing the whole matriarchal world, the relations of the Great Mother Goddess to the world and to man: the earth, the lamb, the child savior, the vulture, Mary, and above them the smiling face of St. Anne surrounded by the spectral blue mountains of the spirit, which dissolve into an ethereal sky.

The conception is not a sacral one; the emphasis seems to be wholly on the human. And herein this painting manifests the secret of the modern world, for which the archetypal symbolism appears to coincide with earthly reality. In the symbol the unity of the earthly and the divine is experienced as human life; and the ancient as well as the medieval cleavage between a higher celestial world and a lower earthly world gives way to a new anthropocentric experience.[114]

Whether Mary was worshiped as a heavenly goddess

114. See my "Bedeutung des Erdarchetyps."

or was regarded as a lower vessel, the earthly genetrix of a God who entered into her from above, in either case the earthly, human middle zone was distinct from the realm of the divine. In Christianity, for this reason, the human was always a prey to sin, needful of grace. But as the human psyche became the scene of divine history, or rather came to be perceived as such, man achieved a new evaluation of the world that we call anthropocentric, because only through such an evaluation do the relation of the divine to the human, the dependency of the divine on the human, become clear.

Leonardo did not reflect on all this; none of it is directly stated in his meditations. But the profane character of his portrayal [115] is compensated by a numinosity of the human, and it is this that fascinates us in his work.

In this new but not yet fully conscious view of the world, the feminine as vehicle of the psychic regains its old rank as the principle that gives birth to life and spirit. For this reason the goddesses with the son, to whom his earthly nature as lamb is subordinated, play a greater part than the Spirit Father of the Middle Ages in determining the new human view of the psyche. In the *St. Anne,* as in nearly all Renaissance madonnas, the son is not the redeeming sacrifice, bleeding on the Cross, forsaken by a cruel God and offered up to mankind, but the "Divine Child" [116] living in the smile of

115. For this reason it is the London *Virgin of the Rocks* with the halo and not the picture in the Louvre that must be regarded as a work of a student.

116. See Jung and Kerényi, *Essays on a Science of Mythology,* pp. 33 ff.

the Mothers, looking up at them, linking the supreme Sophia with the fruit-bringing earth. He plays with the lamb, the childlike animal life of the earth and mankind, which as the good shepherd he will later protect. But even as good shepherd, to whom the flock is entrusted, he remains the beloved son of the Mothers, the bringer of divine salvation, the Spirit-Son of Sophia, who not only holds and shelters the life born of her but also transforms, enhances, and redeems it.

In this Sophia with her mysterious smile there lives the lonely, aging Leonardo's new and supreme experience of Eros. Merejkowski speaks of a drawing in which Mary is shown teaching the little Jesus geometry, and this, I believe, indicates that there is nothing arbitrary or accidental about the relationship we have found between Mona Lisa, St. Anne, and Sophia. From this time on the mysterious smile of Mona Lisa never departs from Leonardo's work; all his remaining paintings are united by the experience of Sophia. The two last among his important paintings, the *John the Baptist* and the closely related *Bacchus,* seem in some mysterious way to develop the motif of the bond between the Divine Son and the Mother.

Leonardo's *John the Baptist* (Pl. V), pointing upward with a mystical smile, as well as the *Bacchus* (Pl. IV), have a puzzling, strangely free and open expression. Even Freud, who, as he himself knew, lacked the "oceanic feeling," and with it the feeling for religion and for any profound art, was captivated by these pictures and expressed this feeling in words that have no parallel in his work: "These pictures breathe a mystical air into whose secret one dares not penetrate."

And further: "The figures are still androgynous, but no longer in the sense of the vulture-phantasy. They are beautiful youths of feminine delicacy and with effeminate forms; they do not cast their eyes down, but gaze in mysterious triumph, as if they knew of a great achievement of happiness, about which silence must be kept. The familiar smile of fascination leads one to guess that it is a secret of love. It is possible that in these figures Leonardo has denied the unhappiness of his erotic life and has triumphed over it in his art, by representing the wishes of the boy, infatuated with his mother, as fulfilled in this blissful union of the male and female natures." [117]

Of Mona Lisa's smile it has been written: "Men call it mysterious, for they stand outside of the woman's bond with the Father God, and it is this bond that calls forth the smile." [118]

This remark does not seem adequate, as is proved by the smile of these divine youths, in whom the Christian and pagan are transcended on a higher plane. Their smile, too, is the symbol of the "love secret" between them and the Great Mother. Both partners in this secret, the young god and the Spirit Mother, are fully entitled to bear the same seal of mystery on their lips. But what does this actually mean? For we know nothing of any

117. *Leonardo*, pp. 117–18.
118. F. du Bois-Reymond, "Über die archetypische Bedingtheit des erstgeborenen Sohnes und seiner Mutter," p. 45.

relationship between John the Baptist and a "mother," and in neither of the two paintings does there seem to be so much as a hint of such a relationship.[119]

The controversy over Leonardo's *Bacchus* leads us to the profound archetypal intention realized in these portrayals of the *puer eternus*. According to one interpretation, the "Bacchus" was originally another "John in the Desert," and the panther skin, vine leaves, and thyrsus were added only at the end of the seventeenth century.[120] Against this thesis Marie Herzfeld writes: "There is no doubt that this poetic composition was always conceived as a Bacchus, since the finding by a contemporary, Flavio Antonio Giraldi, of an epigram in praise of this painting entitled 'Bacchus (!) Leonardi Vinci.' " [121]

The relaxed and indolent way in which the hermaphroditic god sits resting in the countryside is wholly in keeping with the ancient conception of Dionysus. In this picture of the "oriental god," Leonardo, unconsciously no doubt, portrayed a central figure of the matriarchal mystery world, closely related to the vulture goddess. For Dionysus is the mystery god of feminine existence, son of the Phrygian Zemelo, a form of the Great Earth-Mother Goddess of Asia Minor. In Greece the Goddess became the earthly Semele, but even in the

119. The only known connection is characteristically that of the Gospel of St. John, in which Christ on the Cross recommends a mother-son relationship between John the Evangelist and the Madonna.

120. *Tout l'œuvre peint de Leonard de Vinci.*

121. Herzfeld, *op. cit.*

myth of Semele, who dies at the sight of Zeus her lover, the connection between the Virgin Goddess and the masculine Wind-Spirit, the "paternal uroboros," remains discernible.[122] The nymphs and animals that feed Dionysus, as well as his orgies—the ecstatic orgies of the Mother Goddess Cybele,[123] in which man becomes one with nature, and the god is dismembered and eaten in the form of an animal—are expressions of the multiform bond between the young god and the feminine.

Even in antiquity the Dionysian mysteries, which came only late to Greece, were believed to have originated in Egypt, whose goddesses—with Leonardo's vulture goddess at their center—were among the earliest representatives of the Great Mother.

But how can such a Bacchus have passed as a John the Baptist, or, if the painting was originally a Bacchus, how is it that this Bacchus resembles John the Baptist like a twin brother? What a change from the wild desert ascetic to this figure shining with a mysterious inner light! And why the "mysteriously triumphant" look and the mysterious smile of Sophia on his lips?

It is, as Freud dimly saw, the knowledge of a secret union with the Great Mother as mother of all life, the knowledge of the Great Goddess's beloved son that he is forever blessed through his bond with her, through the "blessed union of masculine and feminine being." It is the secret of the matriarchal mysteries, the secret of the immortality of the divine luminous son of the Great

122. Cf. my *Amor and Psyche*, p. 99.
123. Euripides, *The Bacchae*.

71

Mother, resurrected in death.[124] The secret of all her divine sons, bringing redemption and receiving redemption, is one in the mystery smile of St. Anne, of Bacchus, and of John the Baptist.

John crying out in the desert is a symbol of the promise stated in the words of the mystery: "He must increase but I must decrease." John and Christ go together; that is why the festival commemorating the death of St. John occurs at the summer solstice and is celebrated with descending wheels of fire, rolling down the mountains, while the birth of Christ is celebrated at the winter solstice with the kindling of the tree of light, symbol of the newly ascending light. In this sense John and Christ are twin brothers; they are the kindred bearers of light, one of whom in the mysteries of Mithras holds a lowered torch, the other an upraised one, symbols of the falling and the rising light, whose outward sign is the annual course of the sun.

This whole symbolism has its source in the matriarchal sphere, where the Great Mother, the Heavenly Goddess, the vulture goddess, is also the virgin with the ear of light, Demeter-Kore, who in the Eleusinian mysteries bestows the mystery torch, the wheat of heavenly light, upon the masculine, giving it immortality in rebirth.

For the mystery experience of John, John and Christ are one in the exact sense that St. Paul expressed in the words: "I live; yet not I, but Christ liveth in me."

The movement of the hands in the *John the Baptist*

124. Cf. my *Great Mother*, pp. 309 f.

and the *Bacchus* symbolizes the "showing of the secret" in the mysteries. John points upward to the sun of Christ that is rising in him, whose light shines on him from above, while the rest of him is shrouded in darkness. And as John points to the Cross, so Bacchus points to the secret of the thyrsus; while with his other hand, like the youthful John the Baptist in an early study now in the Windsor Library, he points, as though accidentally, downward to the earth. For Bacchus-Dionysus is also a god of life and death, and the rending of Dionysus is a mystery side by side with the crucifixion of Christ and the beheading of John. In Dionysus as in John, ascent is bound up with descent, and both growth and decline are accompanied by the smiling certainty that speaks from their "mysteriously triumphant" gaze, confident of an indissoluble bond with the regenerating Mother of the mysteries.

The hands are always in Leonardo—and not only in the *Last Supper*—essential symbols. The connection between John's upward-pointing hand and St. Anne's identical gesture in the cartoon (Pl. III) is evident. Not only does St. Anne turn with a loving smile to Mary, who is wholly taken up with her love for the Christ child; as Sophia she also admonishes her with her upward-pointed hand: Do not forget, he is not only your child; he belongs to heaven, he is the rising light. If we interpret the otherwise puzzling gesture in this way, the later version of the painting, in which this perhaps too patent indication is lacking, becomes all the more significant; for now this knowledge merges with the higher form of creation that bears its interpretation within itself.[125]

In his attempt to describe the process of individuation,[126] Jung refers to the above-quoted words of St. Paul and remarks that "the center of the total personality no longer coincides with the ego, but with a point midway between the conscious and the unconscious. This would be the point of a new equilibrium, a new centering of the total personality, a virtual center which, on account of its focal position between conscious and unconscious, ensures for the personality a new and more solid foundation."

This process is expressed symbolically in Leonardo's John, with his smile beyond life and death and his knowledge of the waning ego and the waxing self,[127] a knowledge in which the pagan and the Christian are

125. The importance of John for Leonardo, who seems to have taken a profound interest in this figure throughout his life, is reflected by a remarkable and otherwise unintelligible trait in another painting: the strange gesture with which the angel in the incomparably more beautiful Louvre version of *The Virgin of the Rocks* points to the worshiping boy John. It is possible that even then the symbolic contrast between John and Christ, John representing the earthly and human aspect of human nature, Christ the immortal and divine aspect, had become meaningful for Leonardo. Here again we discern Leonardo's "homoerotic" problem, which, as the problem of the archetypal "twins," occurs over and over again in mythology, e.g., the friendship between Gilgamesh and Engidu, between Castor and Pollux, etc.

126. Jung, "The Relations between the Ego and the Unconscious," par. 365.

127. On Christ as a Western symbol, cf. Jung, *Psychology and Alchemy*, "A Psychological Approach to the Dogma of the Trinity," and *Aion*.

joined in a new synthesis. In the Renaissance as in the psychology of modern man, nature, condemned by the Middle Ages, and paganism often appear as symbols of the "contrary aspect" that requires to be integrated. The Christianity of Savonarola and the Inquisition could not but regard Leonardo's John the Baptist as an "alien devil," and it is almost a miracle that Leonardo's paintings survived the religious reaction; but for moderns they are signs and numinous symbols of a new era in modern man's new understanding of himself.

This transcending of good and evil, the Christian and pagan, the masculine and feminine, in Leonardo did not escape Nietzsche's unique psychological insight: "Perhaps Leonardo da Vinci alone of those artists had a really supra-Christian outlook. He knows the East, the 'land of dawn,' within himself as well as without himself. There is something supra-European and silent in him: a characteristic of every one who has seen too wide a circle of things good and bad." [128]

For the experience that took form in Leonardo's picture, Eros and Logos no longer stand in opposition to each other, but form a higher unity. He perceived in the world a mystic unity of creative spontaneity and law, of meaning and necessity. For him love and knowledge had become one.

From this point of view Leonardo recognized that the necessity of death is inherent in nature, just as he had recognized the compensation of nature, who does not leave her creatures "bereft":

128. "Peoples and Countries," *Complete Works,* Vol. 13, pp. 216–17 (modified).

"Why nature did not ordain that one animal should not live by the death of another.

"Nature being inconstant and taking pleasure in creating and making continually new lives and forms, because she knows that they augment her terrestrial substance, is more ready and swift in creating than time is in destroying; and therefore she has ordained that many animals shall serve as food one for the other; and as this does not suffice for her desire she frequently sends forth certain poisonous and pestilential vapors and continual plagues upon the vast accumulations and herds of animals; and most of all upon men, who increase rapidly because other animals do not feed upon them. . . . The earth therefore seeks to lose its life while desiring continual reproduction." [129]

And out of the same feeling for necessity, he wrote: "While I thought that I was learning how to live, I have been learning how to die." [130]

His self-portrait as an old man shows that Leonardo reached a stage of development unique in the West, that of the old sage. But the face in this drawing is not only that of a wise old man; in addition it is the face of a creator and scientist in whom kindness and severity, the torment and restlessness of creation, and the remote serenity of knowledge seem to be balanced. It is strange that among all the faces of "Great Individuals," that of

129. MS. B.M., fol. 156ᵛ. See Herzfeld, p. 133; *Selections,* p. 277.

130. MS. C.A., fol. 252ᵛ. See Herzfeld, p. cxxiii; *Selections,* p. 275.

the aloof and lonely Leonardo should most resemble European man's image of God the Father.

The old sage and the young god are the two archetypal forms in which the masculine is connected with the Great Mother as Sophia. In relation to the young god, the maternal aspect of the Spirit Mother is predominant: he is her son and lover. For the old sage the dominant figure is the young and daughterly Virgin-Sophia; this for Leonardo was Mona Lisa; in her he encountered the Eros of Sophia. Both aspects, which form the totality of the spiritual feminine, were effective for Leonardo to the end of his life; in relation to them he remained problematic and ambivalent: youth and old sage at once.

Leonardo's lifelong fidelity to the figure of the vulture goddess, to which every phase of his creative existence bears witness, was the actual reason for his loneliness, never broken by any human proximity.[131]

His love and his Eros exceeded the limits of the

131. That the archetypal picture of the vulture goddess, of the feminine fecundated by the masculine spirit-wind, never ceased to grow in him is also reflected in the fact that one of his last works, preserved in a drawing and in a student's copy, was a picture of Leda and the Swan. Impregnated by the bird-wind, Leda is the mother of the hero. She too discloses the smile, bearing witness to the woman's bond with the Father God. At her feet play the children born of the egg, and the egg always symbolized the offspring of the Great Mother. These children are Castor and Pollux, who, in antiquity, like John and Christ, embody the twin, mortal and immortal, nature of the hero. Some copies show beside them the daughters of the egg, Helen and Clytemnestra, the matriarchal representatives of the seductive and the killing aspects of the Great Mother, so dangerous to the masculine.

77

human. That was his greatness and at the same time his limitation. His Eros never forsook its bond with the infinite, the mother goddess. What in the beginning was an unconscious motive became in the course of his life a reality, the reality of his works and scientific investigations, and at last, in his middle years, resulted in the human encounter with Mona Lisa. But it was no accident that this encounter was with a woman doomed soon to die: even in his human dealings he preserved his bond with the infinite.

He had written these radical, misanthropic words: "While you are alone you are entirely your own; and if you have but one companion, you are but half your own, and even less in proportion to the indiscretion of his conduct. And if you have more companions, you will fall deeper into the same trouble. If you should say, 'I will go my own way, I will withdraw apart the better to study the forms of natural objects,' I tell you that this will work badly because you cannot help often lending an ear to their chatter." [132]

But this attitude was not that of the solitary, brooding eccentric. Vasari had written of Leonardo: "By the splendor of his magnificent union he comforted every sad soul, and his eloquence could turn men to either side of the question." [133]

Not bitter hatred of man, as with Michelangelo, but devotion to the inner forces guiding his existence was at the bottom of this aloofness so uncommon in the frantically convivial Renaissance. But he was perfectly capable

132. From the *Traktat von der Malerei; Selections*, pp. 216–17.
133. *Lives of the Painters*, Vol. III, p. 327.

of love and affection; witness the profound attachment of his pupil Melzi, who accompanied Leonardo to France and remained with him to the day of his death:

"To me he was like the best of fathers," he wrote, "for whose death it would be impossible for me to express the grief I have felt; and so long as these my links endure I shall possess a perpetual sorrow, and with good reason, since he showed to me day by day the warmest love and devotion. It is a hurt to anyone to lose such a man, for nature cannot again produce his like." [134]

Yet in spite of all this he was always closer to the infinite than to the finite, and in a mysterious, symbolic way his life was lived in the myth of the Great Goddess. For him the figure of the Spirit Father, of the great demiurge and fecundating wind god, always remained secondary to the Great Goddess, who had chosen the child in the cradle and showered him with her gifts, who spread her spirit wings over his life as she spread them over the world. For Leonardo the yearning to return to her, his source and home, was the yearning not only of his own life, but of the life of the whole world.

"Behold, the hope and the desire of going back to one's country [*repatriarsi*] and of returning to the primal state of chaos is like that of the moth to the light, and of the man who with perpetual longing looks forward with joy to each new spring and to each new summer, and to the new months and the new years, deeming that the things he looks for are too slow in coming; and he does not perceive that he is longing for his own destruction. But this longing is in its quintessence the spirit of

134. *Selections*, p. 392.

the elements, which finding itself imprisoned as the soul within the human body is ever longing to return to its sender; and I would have you know that this same longing is that quintessence inherent in nature, and that man is a type of the world." [135]

Thus the star of the Great Mother is the central star in Leonardo's sky. It shines over his cradle as over his death. The same goddess who appeared to the unconscious child in his cradle becomes St. Anne, the supreme spiritual and psychic incarnation of the feminine smiling down upon the Christ child. As earth and nature, she was the object of his researches; as art and wisdom she was the goddess of his transformations. Preserving a balance almost unique among Western men, Leonardo, in a process of unremitting self-discipline, fused his many gifts into a higher unity. He halted at no stage of development, but passed through the world as though from the very start his inner eye had perceived the constellation to which his way and life led him, the constellation of the mother goddess, protectress of his childhood, home of his old age. His life was the realization of the maxim that he recorded in one of his notebooks:

"He who fixes his course by a star changes not." [136]

135. MS. B.M., fol. 156ᵛ; *Selections,* p. 276.
136. R. 682, MS. W.L., fol. 198ʳ. See Herzfeld, p. 141; Mac-Curdy, Vol. I, p. 99.

# II

## ART AND TIME

Art and time is a vast theme; I am sure you do not expect an exhaustive treatment of it in one lecture. Here we shall not concern ourselves with the phenomenon of time as it enters into man's experience or into his actual works of art; in other words, we shall not concern ourselves with the relation of the ego to the living stream of time, to eternity or the moment, to the swirling eddies of time, or to repose in time. Our discussion will deal principally with the relation of art to its epoch; the second part of our lecture will take up the specific relation of modern art to our own time.

However, I shall speak neither as an artist nor as an art critic; I shall not even speak of the artistic phenomena with which I come into contact as a psychologist, the more or less artistic productions that arise in the course of analytical therapy. Our present inquiry lies within the psychology of culture; it aims at an understanding of art as a psychological phenomenon of central importance to the collectivity as well as the individual.

We shall start from the creative function of the unconscious, which produces its forms spontaneously, in a manner analogous to nature, which—from atom and crystal through organic life to the world of the stars and planets—spontaneously creates forms susceptible of impressing man as beautiful. Because this substratum and background of the psychophysical world is forever bringing forth forms, we call it creative. And to the unknown in nature which engenders its forms of the external world there corresponds another unknown, the collective unconscious, which is the source of all psychic creation: religion and rite, social organization, consciousness, and finally art.

The archetypes of the collective unconscious are intrinsically formless psychic structures which become visible in art. The archetypes are varied by the media through which they pass—that is, their form changes according to the time, the place, and the psychological constellation of the individual in whom they are manifested. Thus, for example, the mother archetype, as a dynamic entity in the psychic substratum, always retains its identity, but it takes on different *styles*—different aspects or emotional color—depending on whether it is manifested in Egypt, Mexico, or Spain, or in ancient, medieval, or modern times. The paradoxical multiplicity of its eternal presence, which makes possible an infinite variety of forms of expression, is crystallized in its realization by man in time; its archetypal eternity enters into a unique synthesis with a specific historical situation.

Today we shall neither inquire into the development of specific archetypes in *one* culture nor follow the different forms of the same archetype in diverse cultures. Anyone wishing to convince himself of the reality of this overwhelming phenomenon need only consult the Eranos Archive,[1] a pioneer effort in this direction.

Nor shall we take up the aesthetic aspect, the history of styles, which inquires into the forms assumed by the archetypes in the various periods, although it would be exceedingly interesting to show, for example, how the archetypal world of Egypt was shaped by a static conception of eternity and time, while in Central America the same archetypal world is almost submerged in a jungle of ornament because here the all-devouring aspect of the Terrible Mother is dominant. Our effort will begin and end with the question of what art means for mankind and what position it occupies in human development.

At the beginning of the development of human consciousness the original psychic situation prevails: unconscious, collective, and transpersonal factors are more significant and evident than conscious and individual factors. Art is at this stage a collective phenomenon, which cannot be isolated from the context of collective existence but is integrated with the life of the group. Each individual is artist, dancer, singer, poet, painter, and sculptor; everything he does and his way of doing it, even where a recognized individual possession is involved, remains an expression of the group's effective situation.

Although from the very outset the collective receives its primary impulse from "Great Individuals," even they themselves, in accordance with the dialectic of their re-

1. [At the Warburg Institute, London. A duplicate is incorporated in the Archive for Research in Archetypal Symbolism, New York.—ED.]

lation to the group, never give themselves as individuals credit for what they have done but impute it to their inspiring predecessors, to the spirits of their ancestors, to the totem, or to whatever aspect of the collective spirit has inspired them individually.

Not only *is* the creative situation numinous; it is also experienced as such, for all existence was originally shaped by experience of the transpersonal. The festivals and rites are the nodal points of the numinosum, which shapes everything that comes into contact with its sacral sphere: cult implement and mask, figure and image, vessel and ornament, song and dance, myth and poetry. The original integration of all these into life and the numinous context as a whole is shown by the fact that a certain "style" is Oceanic or African, Indian or Nordic, and that it is manifested in the kinship between ornamented door post and ritual vessel, between tattoo motif and mask, fetish and spear shaft.

This unity is a symptom of the individual's immersion in a group context that transcends him; however, when we say that the group is unconsciously directed by the collective psyche, we do not mean that it is directed by urges or instincts. True, the individual's consciousness is almost blind to the underlying forces: his reaction to the creative impulse of the psyche is not to reflect; it is to obey and execute its commands. But the psychic undercurrents which determine man's feeling and image of the world are manifested through colors and forms, tones and words, which crystallize into symbolic spiritual figures expressing man's relation both to the archetypal world and to the world in which he lives.

Thus from the very outset man is a creator of symbols; he constructs his characteristic spiritual-psychic world from the symbols in which he speaks and thinks of the world around him, but also from the forms and images which his numinous experience arouses in him.

In the original situation man's emotion in the presence of the numinosum leads to expression, for the unconscious, as part of its creative function, carries with it its own expression. But the emotional drives which move the group and the individual within it must not be conceived as a dynamic without content. For every symbol, like every archetype, has a specific content, and when the whole of a man is seized by the collective unconscious, that means his consciousness too. Consequently we find from the very start that the creative function of the psyche is accompanied by a reaction of consciousness, which seeks, at first in slight degree but then increasingly, to understand, to interpret, and to assimilate the thing by which it was at first overwhelmed. Thus at a very early stage there is a relative fixation of expression and style, and so definite traditions arise.

In our time, with its developed or overdeveloped consciousness, feeling and emotion seem to be bound up with an artistic nature; for an undeveloped consciousness this is by no means the case. For primitive and early cultures, the creative force of the numinosum supports or even engenders consciousness: it brings differentiation and order into an indeterminate world driven by chaotic powers and enables man to orient himself.

In the creative sphere of the psyche, which we call the unconscious, significant differentiations have been effected in the direction which will be characteristic of subsequent elaborations by consciousness. The very appearance of a psychic image represents a synthetic interpretation of the world, and the same is true of artistic creation in the period of origination. Artistic creation has magic power; it is experience and perception, insight and differentiation in one.

Whether the image is naturalistic or not is immaterial; even the extremely naturalistic animal paintings of the Ice Age are, in our sense, symbols. For a primitive, magical conception of the world, each of these painted animals is a numinosum; it is the embodiment and essence of the animal species. The individual bison, for example, is a spiritual-psychic symbol; he is in a sense the "father of the bison," the idea of the bison, the "bison as such," and this is why he is an object of ritual. The subjugation and killing, the conciliation and fertilization of the animal, which are enacted in the psychic sphere between the human group and the image that symbolically represents the animal group, have a reality-transforming —that is, magical—significance, because this image symbol encompasses the numinous heart and center of the animal living in the world, whose symbolic figuration constitutes an authentic manifestation of the numinous animal.

In the period of origination, the forms of expression and driving archetypal contents of a culture remain unconscious; but with the development and systematization of consciousness and the reinforcement of the individual ego there arises a collective consciousness, a cultural canon characteristic for each culture and cultural epoch.

There arises, in other words, a configuration of definite archetypes, symbols, values, and attitudes, upon which the unconscious archetypal contents are projected and which, fixated as myth and cult, becomes the dogmatic heritage of the group. No longer do unconscious and unknown powers determine the life of the group; instead, transpersonal figures and contents, known to the group, direct the life of the community as well as the conscious behavior of the individual in festival and cult, religion and usage.

This does not mean that man suspects a connection between this transpersonal world and the depths of his own human psyche, although the transpersonal can express itself only through the medium of man and takes form in him through creative processes.

But even when the cultural canon develops, art in all its forms remains at first integrated with the whole of the group life, and when the cultural canon is observed in religious festival, all creative activity is articulated with this integral event. As expressions of archetypal reality, the art and music, dance and poetry of the cult are inner possessions of the collective.

Whether the epiphany of the numinosum occurs in a drawing scratched on bone, in a sculptured stone, in a medieval cathedral centuries in the building, or in a mask, fashioned for *one* festival and burned after it, in every case the epiphany of the numinosum, the rapture of those who give it form, and the rapture of the group celebrating the epiphany constitute an indivisible unit.

But the breakdown of this original situation in the course of history is revealed also by the phenomenon of the individual creator in art. With the growth of individuality and the relative independence of consciousness, the integral situation in which the creative element in art is one with the life of the group disintegrates. An extensive differentiation occurs; poets, painters, sculptors, musicians, dancers, actors, architects, etc., become professional groups, practicing particular functions of artistic expression. The majority of the group, it would appear, preserves only a receptive relation, if any, to the creative achievement of the artist.

But neither is the individual so isolated—nor are art and the artist so far separated—from the collective as first appears. We have learned to see the consciousness of the individual as the high voice in a polyphony whose lower voice, the collective unconscious, does not merely accompany but actually determines the theme. And this reorientation is not limited to the psychic structure of the individual; it also necessitates a new approach to the relations between men.

We see the group as an integral psychic field, in which the reality of the individual is embedded, so that he is organ and instrument of the collective. But not only through his consciousness or his education by the collective is the individual embedded in this psychic field. The separate structures of the human organism regulate one another in a highly complex way, and in dreams those structures necessary for the whole of the individual personality are animated in such a way as to compensate for the one-sidedness of conscious life; similarly, there exists between the members of a group a compensatory mechanism which—quite apart from the directives of the

individual consciousness and of the cultural authorities
—tends to round out the group life.

In the group as in the individual, two psychic systems
are at work, which can function smoothly only when
they are attuned to each other. The one is the collective
consciousness, the cultural canon, the system of the culture's supreme values toward which its education is
oriented and which set their decisive stamp on the development of the individual consciousness. But side by
side with this is the living substratum, the collective unconscious, in which new developments, transformations,
revolutions, and renewals are at all times foreshadowed
and prepared and whose perpetual eruptions prevent the
stagnation and death of a culture. But even if we see the
group as an integral psychic field, the men in whom
reside the compensatory unconscious forces necessary to
the cultural canon and the culture of the particular time
are also essential elements of this constellation. However, only the historian—and he, too, is limited by his
personal equation and his ties with his epoch—can eval-
uate the authentic historical significance of a group, a
movement, or an individual. For there is no necessary
relation between the true importance of a man and that
imputed to him by his own time—that is, by the representatives of his own cultural canon. In the course of
time, "leaders" and "geniuses" are exposed as frauds,
while outsiders, outlaws, nobodies, are found to have
been the true vehicles of reality.

Not the ego and consciousness but the collective unconscious and the self are the determining forces; the
development of man and his consciousness is dependent

on the spontaneity and the inner order of the unconscious and remains so even after consciousness and unconscious have entered into a fruitful dialectical relation to each other.

There is a continuous interchange between the collective unconscious (which is alive in the unconscious of every individual in the group), the cultural canon (which represents the group's collective consciousness of those archetypal values which have become dogma), and the creative individuals of the group (in whom the new constellations of the collective unconscious achieve form and expression).[2]

Our attempt to distinguish different forms of relation between art and the artist and their epoch is based upon the unity of the group's psychic field, in which, consciously or unconsciously, willingly or unwillingly, every single individual, and every sphere of culture as well, takes its place.[3] This unity—like that of the individual psyche—is composed of collective consciousness and collective unconscious.

2. We must leave out of account here the fact that the same constellations may appear in Great Individuals and in borderline cases of neurosis and insanity.

3. The psychological evaluation of the individual within the group as a whole presents an analogy to his sociological position. But the two evaluations, as we have stressed, can be utterly divergent. Since an insight into these compensatory relations is necessary to an estimate of the individual's importance to the community, we must, in judging the individual, use the notion of "social adaptation" much more cautiously than was previously the case when—quite understandably—adaptation to the values of the cultural canon was regarded as the sole criterion. The dilemma that this circumstance creates for depth psychology in its relation to the collective cannot be discussed here.

The first stage in the relation of art to its epoch is, as we have suggested, the self-representation of the unconscious in the symbolic expression of the numinosum, characteristic of the situation of origination and of early cultures. The self-representation of the unconscious in art always presupposes a greater or lesser degree of unity, whether conscious or not, in the creative man's personality; and it presupposes that he must be embedded in his group. Moreover, the product of this phase is also characterized by unity; it is an art integrated with the group as a whole.

In the representation of the cultural canon, the second stage in the relation of art to its epoch, this is no longer the case. And here it is immaterial whether it is an ancestor, a god, or a Buddha who appears in the cultural canon, and whether it is the awakening of Osiris, a crucifixion, or the cutting out of the god's heart that figures as a part of the savior myth.

Such canonical forms are, of course, also grounded in archetypes; that is, even in its representative form, art is a symbolic expression of the collective unconscious and, although it is essentially a representation of symbols close to consciousness, it has a decisive therapeutic function for the life of the group. For the fact that the symbol is consciously represented does not necessarily mean that it has been made fully conscious or that it has been dissolved through conscious assimilation.

True, the representation of the archetype in a cultural canon is closer to consciousness than the pure self-representation of the unconscious; the numinous power becomes less unknown. But because every symbol also expresses an essential unknown component of the psyche, its unconscious workings continue for a long time, even when it is interpreted and understood as part of the cultural canon.

Thus in all cultures the archetypes of the canon are the numinous points at which the collective unconscious extends into the living reality of the group.[4] Whether this be a temple or a statue of the godhead, a mask or a fetish, a ritual or sacral music, it remains the function of art to represent the archetypal and to manifest it symbolically as a high point of existence.

This artistic representation of the cultural canon resembles the digging and walling in of deep wells, around which the group gathers and from whose waters it lives. Every such well is adorned with traditional symbols in which lives the religious consciousness of the epoch.

But the cultural canon is not only a bond with the archetypal substratum of the unconscious. As "canon" it is also a means of limiting and fixating the intervention of the numinosum and excluding unpredictable creative forces. Thus the cultural canon is always a fortress of security; and since it is a systematic restriction to a dogmatic section of the numinosum, it carries with it the danger of one-sidedness and congealment. For the archetypal world is a dynamic world of change, and even the numinosum and the divine are mortal in the contingent form which can be apprehended by man.

The archetypal as such is imageless and nameless, and the form which the formless assumes at any time is, as an image arising in the medium of man, transient. And

4. Cf. my *Origins and History of Consciousness*, pp. 371–75.

just as the archetypal cultural canon must arise and take form, so likewise its representation is transient and must undergo change and transformations.

For the artist, whose vocation it is to represent the cultural canon, it is a question of growing into a tradition—that is, into the situation of his time and into the collective consciousness—rather than of receiving a direct mandate from the powers of the unconscious. Of course, an image of the canon can also be full of inner experience, but its archetypal reality may no longer encompass the whole of the artistic personality. An art which is oriented toward those sectors of the archetypal world that have already entered into consciousness through representation will never realize the supreme possibilities of art.

However, the creative process need not consist of an outward shattering of the cultural canon; it can operate underground, within the canon. Accordingly, the object depicted in a work of art cannot tell us whether we have to do with a representation of the cultural canon or with an evolution or revolution from it. If, within the Christian canon that has dominated the West for nearly two thousand years, we compare a Gothic, a Renaissance, and a modern Madonna, we see at once the revolutionary transformation of this archetypal figure. And a Byzantine Christ-Pantocrator and Grünewald's Christ on the Cross have their source in different worlds of God and man. One might almost say that they were no longer related.

The next stage in the relation of art to its epoch is the stage of compensation for the cultural canon, and the significance of this has repeatedly been stressed by Professor Jung.[5] It is grounded in the vitality of the collective unconscious, which is opposed to the collective consciousness in the integral psychic field of the group. This stage presupposes the existence of an established opposition of consciousness to the unconscious, characteristic of the modern world. In it we go back to the immediate presence of the creative numinosum. Great art of this type almost necessarily implies tragedy. Compensation for the cultural canon means opposition to it —that is, opposition to the epoch's consciousness and sense of values. The creative artist, whose mission it is to compensate for consciousness and the cultural canon, is usually an isolated individual, a hero who must destroy the old in order to make possible the dawn of the new.

When unconscious forces break through in the artist, when the archetypes striving to be born into the light of the world take form in him, he is as far from the men around him as he is close to their destiny. For he expresses and gives form to the future of his epoch.

For example, the realism which emerged in Renaissance painting and which for centuries dominated our art has a significance far beyond such purely artistic considerations as mobility of the figure, perspective, plasticity, color, etc. Renaissance art did not, as it might appear, abandon medieval symbolism in order to reproduce the objective outside world; what actually took place—and it is a phenomenon decisive for this epoch—was the re-

5. Cf. especially his articles on Picasso and the novel *Ulysses*.

appearance of the earth archetype, in opposition to the heaven archetype that had dominated the Middle Ages. In other words, this naturalism is the symbolic expression of a revolution in the archetypal structure of the unconscious.

The beginning of natural science and sociology, the discovery of the individual and of classical antiquity, the schism in Christianity, the social revolution, etc., are all a part of the integral transformation of the psychic field, which seized upon the unconscious of all men—particularly of creative men. Thus a Dutch genre painting is not merely a representation of a fragment of external reality; it is a glorification of this world as opposed to the next, a discovery of the sanctity, the beauty, and the vitality of the material world, a praise of life in this world and of earthly man, in opposition to the praise of heaven, which had hitherto passed for the "real" world.

And whereas man's relation to this transcendent "real" world had led to a life burdened with original sin, with a sense of guilt and eternal inadequacy, man now came to feel that he was a son of the earth, at home on earth.

This intense conflict governed the work of Bosch, one of the most magnificent painters ever to have announced the coming of a new era.[6] He clung consciously to the old medieval canon, but beneath his hand the world transformed itself. It became demonic and gnostic;

6. See Wilhelm Fränger, *The Millennium of Hieronymus Bosch: Outlines of a New Interpretation.* I have intentionally avoided consideration of Fränger's interpretations, since it is impossible to judge at the present moment to what degree they are tenable.

everything was temptation, and in the paranoiac despair of his ascetic, medieval consciousness he experienced the revival of the earth archetype around him, glittering demonically in every color. Paradoxically enough, although, and precisely because, for him Satan—in the form of an owl—had stood from the very first at the heart of creation, his earth transformed itself into an "earthly paradise." And all the colors and forms of this ostensibly accursed earthly paradise shine alluringly in a wealth of archetypal and classical ritual symbols, with such beauty that, although he himself did not know it, the curse, like Balaam's, has turned unexpectedly to blessing.

In his attempt to represent the demon-infested earth in the earthly colors of his unique palette, the earth magnificently triumphed over his medieval conception. Consequently, for example, his *Christ Bearing the Cross* (Pl. VI), and the Veronica in this painting, disclose nothing medieval but on the contrary point to one of the most modern problems of future generations: the Great Individual with his soul, alone in the mass of men.

The workings of this ascendant earth archetype, which was to become a central component of the new cultural canon, extended down to the French Revolution, to philosophical materialism, and to the Madonna's rather belated dogmatic assumption into heaven. Only today has this process begun to be intelligible, but concurrently this archetype is beginning in turn to undergo a transformation: the projection is being dissolved and the content reintegrated into the psyche. As one of the greatest poets of our time has written:

> Earth, isn't this what you want: an invisible
> re-arising in us? Is it not your dream
> to be one day invisible? Earth! invisible!
> What is your urgent command, if not transformation?
> Earth, you darling, I will! [7]

The need of his times works inside the artist without his wanting it, seeing it, or understanding its true significance. In this sense he is close to the seer, the prophet, the mystic. And it is precisely when he does not represent the existing canon but transforms and overturns it that his function rises to the level of the sacral, for he then gives utterance to the authentic and direct revelation of the numinosum.

The advance of specialization and differentiation has destroyed the closeness of every individual to the psychic substratum, characteristic of the original situation. Since culture is in part a safeguard against the numinosum, the representatives of the cultural canon have lost contact with the primal fire of direct inner experience. Nor is this inner experience their function, for they represent the conscious and rational aspect of the archetypal world, the striving to safeguard and secure the artificial, cultural shell of life. Consequently, the creative struggle with the numinosum has fallen to the lot of the individual, and an essential arena of this struggle is art, in which the relation of the creative individual to the numinosum takes form.

In following the drive of the psychic substratum, the artist fulfills not only himself but also his epoch. In the

7. R. M. Rilke, *Duino Elegies* (tr. Leishman and Spender), IX, p. 87.

original situation the artist, or any person proposing to shape a cult object, had to cleanse himself in order to achieve an exalted and detached transpersonal state, in which alone he could become the creative instrument of the powers. In the original situation this ritual preparation was undertaken in accord with the collective. To the modern artist it happens involuntarily; an outsider in society, he stands alone, delivered over to the creative impulse in himself.

We know that the creative power of the unconscious seizes upon the individual with the autonomous force of an instinctual drive and takes possession of him without the least consideration for the individual, his life, his happiness, or his health. The creative impulse springs from the collective; like every instinct it serves the will of the species and not of the individual. Thus the creative man is an instrument of the transpersonal, but as an individual he comes into conflict with the numinosum that takes hold of him.

Creative phenomena range from the lowest, unconscious stages of ecstatic frenzy and somnambulism to the highest level of conscious acceptance, in which the artist takes full responsibility and a formative, interpreting consciousness plays an essential part.

A similar conflict dominates the relation of the artist to his collective and his time. If he is driven to compensate for the cultural canon, there is an implication that he has been captured by it and has survived and transcended it in himself. Only by suffering, perhaps unconsciously, under the poverty of his culture and his time can he arrive at the freshly opening source which is destined to quench the thirst of his time. In other words, the creative man (though often this is not evident) is deeply bound up with his group and its culture, more deeply than the common man who lives in the security of the cultural shell, and even more deeply than the actual representatives of this culture.

And because of the predominance of the transpersonal in the psychic substratum of creative men, their psychic field is integral. For although creative men usually live unknown to one another, without influence on one another, a common force seems to drive all those men who ever compensate for a cultural canon at a given time or shape a new one. They are all moved in the same direction, though they follow an unknown impulse in themselves rather than any new road charted in advance. This phenomenon is called simply *Zeitgeist,* and no further attempt is made to account for it.

At a later day we can analyze and set up all sorts of chains of causality to explain the *Zeitgeist,* but these explanations after the fact are only in part convincing. Perhaps the least presumptuous of them states that the force which breaks through at one and the same time in philosophy and literature, painting and music, science and politics, and in innumerable creative individuals— the force that sets its imprint on the spirit of a time, of *any* time—is transpersonal and unconscious. Here again we do not wish to underestimate the role of the consciousness that responds to conscious problems, but we must attach great significance, crucial significance, to the directives of the collective unconscious.

In all these stages in the relation of art to its time—

self-representation of the unconscious, representation of the cultural canon, and compensation for the cultural canon—the psychic field in which the individual is embedded remains the decisive factor. Despite all the changes brought about in the course of human development, the individual's relation to the collective remains his destiny.

But in the course of human history the artist becomes constantly more individualized and loses his original anonymity. As the ego and consciousness develop, the physiognomy of the individual artist is liberated from the anonymity of the current style. This individualization of creative man is the beginning of his individuation —that is, of the last form of relation between art and its epoch.

We shall designate this last phase as the transcendence of art. It rests, we believe, on an individual development of the artist, which makes him into the Great Individual who, precisely, transcends his bond with the collective both outwardly and inwardly. It is no longer his function to express the creative will of the unconscious or to depict a sector of the archetypal world, or to regenerate or compensate for the existing culture out of the depths of the collective unconscious.

What is fundamentally new and different in this stage is that the artist here attains to the level of timelessness. And reluctant as we are to use such terms, this stage of artistic creation cannot be characterized without such words as "eternity," "intuition of essence" (*Wesensschau*), and "metaphysical experience."

Although every creative representation of an arche-

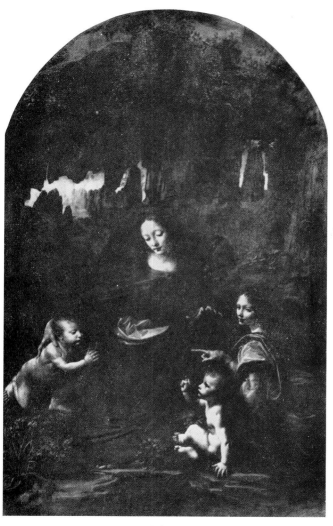

LEONARDO DA VINCI: The Virgin of the Rocks

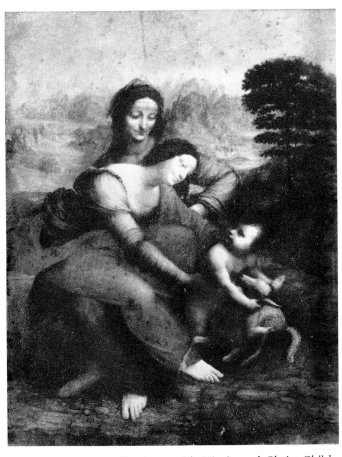

LEONARDO DA VINCI: St. Anne with Virgin and Christ Child

II

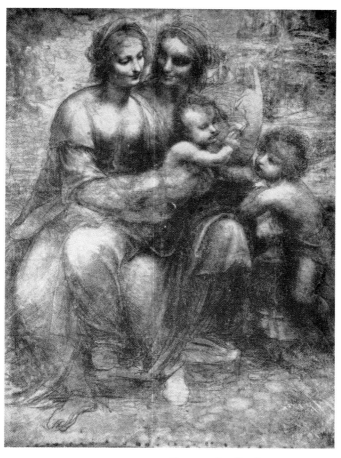

LEONARDO DA VINCI: Cartoon for St. Anne

III

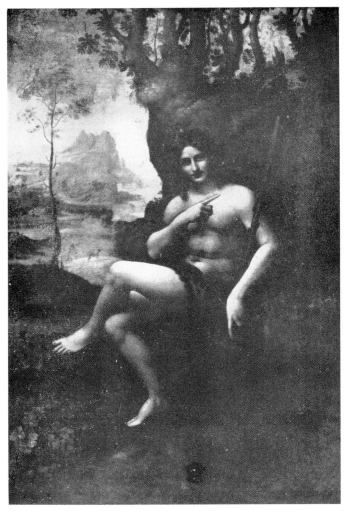

LEONARDO DA VINCI: Bacchus

IV

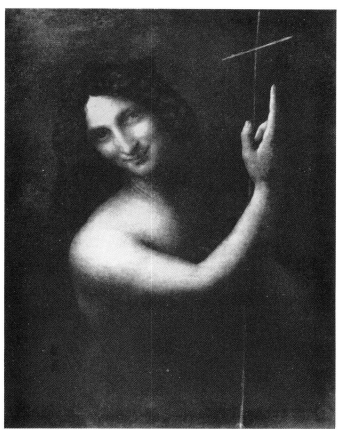

LEONARDO DA VINCI: John the Baptist

V

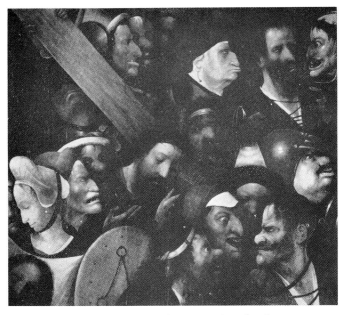

HIERONYMUS BOSCH: Christ Bearing the Cross

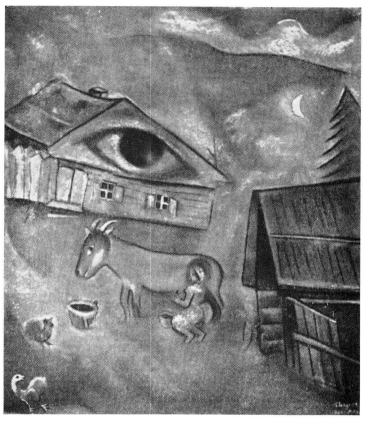

MARC CHAGALL: The Green Eye

VII

type is a representation of something eternal, and although the archetypes are the real content of art, the eternal quality in a work of art can by no means be apprehended at first glance. Precisely because art is devoted to such a great extent to the representation of the cultural canon, its understanding requires historical knowledge, an orientation in the assumptions of the cultural canon to which the work belongs. Here perhaps you will disagree, but consider how we take the greatness of Asian or primitive art for granted today, and then recall Goethe's judgment on the horrid idols of India and the general opinion of primitives held up to a generation ago. Only in our own time has it become possible to experience and appreciate a "world art."

And consider that nearly all the great artists of our own culture, from Rembrandt to Bach, from the Gothic sculptors to El Greco, have had to be rediscovered. Here, too, we are the heirs of a tradition which taught us to see, hear, and experience anew. Where there is new knowledge of man, new art will be discovered, and the eternal in the art of the past will be discovered afresh.

In this sense, the timelessness of art can be experienced only by an enhanced consciousness, for what figure of Christ can be fully understood without knowledge of Christianity, what Buddha without Buddhism, what Shiva without the Hindu conception of cosmic cycles?

Is, then, the stage of transcendent art an illusion? Can we really know nothing more than the relation of the work of art to ourselves and to its own time? And is the most we can say of an artist that, if we disregard the eternity of the archetype he represented, he was a hair's breadth in advance of his own time?

Perhaps I can best explain what I mean by "transcendent" if I refer to the works of the great artists' old age.

We are accustomed—and this, too, is an acquisition of the last Western century, with its emphasis on the individual—to take an interest in the biographies of artists. We approach their lives like the mythological lives of prehistoric heroes, except that these Great Individuals are closer to us and we feel more related to their sufferings and victories, so that, far above us as they may be, they seem to offer a pledge of the dignity of our own individual existence.

It is no idle curiosity that makes us follow the course of their lives. They serve us as models in the sense that their work and lives form the unity which we call individuation and for which we must strive on the smaller scale allotted to us.

Each of these artists seems to pass through all the stages that we have attempted to characterize. He begins by responding to a creative impulse within him, which, as in the stage of the self-expression of the unconscious, strives to find form of whatever kind. Then, maturing, he grows into the contingency of his epoch; through study, he becomes the heir and son of his cultural tradition.

But whether the artist grows slowly away from the tradition of his time or passes over it at one bound and brings the new element the epoch lacked, ultimately, if he does not stop at the stage of representation of the cultural canon—and no truly great artist has ever done so—he finds himself alone. He is alone regardless of whether he is worshiped as an Olympian, whether he is an organist respected in a small circle, or whether he ends in deafness, poverty, or madness.

The struggle of these great men with the powers inside them and the times outside them seems to result in a statement which transcends the artistic and symbolic reality of their creative life. In music, painting, sculpture, and poetry they penetrate to the archetypal transcendence which is the inner life of the world. What speaks to us from a self-portrait of the aged Rembrandt, from the end of *Faust,* Part II, from Shakespeare's last plays or Titian's late paintings, from *The Art of Fugue* or a late Beethoven quartet, is a strange transfiguration, a break-through into the realm of essence. And this transfiguration is independent of content, form, matter, or style, although the transcendence of form would seem to be one of its elements.

In these works of man a numinous world is manifested in which the polarity of outward and inward—nature and art—seems to be resolved. Their secret alchemy achieves a synthesis of the numinosum at the heart of nature and psyche.

These aged masters seem to have attained the image and likeness of a primal creative force, prior to the world and outside the world, which, though split from the very beginning into the polarity of nature and psyche, is in essence one undivided whole.

In the creative solitude of the Great Old Men the limitations of the epoch are passed over; they have escaped the prison of time and the ego-bound consciousness. We begin to see that the supreme alchemical transformation of art merely reflects the alchemical transformation of the Great Individual's personality. At first, whether carried along by the powers or resisting them, he had remained distinct from them. But now, as his ego itself is integrated by the creative self, which from the very outset was the directing force of his existence, the center of gravity shifts. The original tension between his ego, the numinous substratum, and the outside world is annulled and, in the highest form of this transcending art, replaced by a creative act which is spirit-nature and transfigured nature.

For this reason it is not possible to characterize the style of these works of advanced age, for the creative integration of the personality transcends the contingency of any time-bound form.

This art no longer relates either consciously or unconsciously to any historical time; the solitary monologue of these "extreme" works is spoken, as it were, into the void. And one cannot quite tell whether it is a monologue or a dialogue between man and the ultimate. Hence the alienation of these great men from their contemporaries—they all, like the aged Laotse, have left the mountain pass of the world behind them.

If we call this transcendent art religious it is because the faith of Bach and the atheistic infinity of a Chinese landscape would seem to be two kindred forms of transcendence, and because we regard these ultimate works and many others of different kinds as the supreme religious act of which creative mankind is capable.

And here again we must declare that a feeling for this universal kinship has become possible only in our own ostensibly irreligious time, a time, as we often hear, that is fit only to be destroyed. Wherever traditional art apprehends the essence of the archetype, it does so by fitting the archetype into a fixed framework oriented toward the human world—even when this archetype consists of the death of the Saviour, the meditation of the Buddha, or the emanation of the divine. As object of worship, as example, and as representation of the transpersonal, it always signifies a descent of the eternal into the reality of a secure world of faith.

But in the rare instances when the phenomenon of transcendence occurs, the transpersonal seems, even though it has passed through the medium of the human, to have achieved its own objectivity—to speak, one might say, with itself. It is no longer oriented toward the world or man, the ego or the collective, security or insecurity; instead, the creative act which mysteriously creates form and life in nature as in the human psyche seems to have perceived itself and to shine forth with its own incandescence. The creative impulse seems to have liberated itself. United on the plane of artistic creation, the self which man experiences within him and the world-creative self which is manifested outwardly achieve the transparency of symbolic reality.

Of course, it is impossible to state objectively that everyone can find this transcendence in certain specific works of art. It suffices to note that the level exists and it is possible to experience it in some works of art. One of us will find it in a landscape by Leonardo or a poem by Goethe; another will find it elsewhere. But in any event we may say that this experience can be gained only through a few of the very greatest works and only by those who are open and prepared for it. For even when the highest form of artistic reality has achieved objective existence in a work, it must be reborn in subjective human experience.

And it seems to us that one of the principal functions of all art is precisely to set in motion the archetypal reality of the transpersonal within the individual and on the highest level of artistic experience to bring the individual himself to transcendence—that is, to raise him above time and epoch and also above the limited eternity realized in any limited archetypal form—to lead him to the timeless radiant dynamic that is at the heart of the world.

In this sense the greatest art is a learning to see in the way described by Rabbi Nachman of Bratislava: "Just as a hand ·held before the eyes conceals the greatest mountain, so does petty earthly life conceal from view the vast lights and mysteries of which the world is full, and he who can withdraw it from his eyes, as one withdraws a hand, will behold the great light of the innermost world." [8]

II

It is difficult if not impossible to analyze the art of our own time, because we ourselves still live entirely within the psychic field of which it is a part. You will therefore

8. Martin Buber, *Die chassidischen Bücher,* p. 32.

forgive me for returning briefly to matters we have already touched upon.

In Fig. 2, you will find a diagram of a "balanced" culture, showing a collectivity and an epoch integrated with a cultural canon. The semicircle is the arch supporting the supreme values of the time, the symbols, images, ideals that constitute the transpersonal medium in which the psychic-spiritual existence of the collectivity is rooted. An archetype of the collective unconscious is associated with each of these supreme values. And we may say that the depth and force of an archetype, which is perceived through its projection into a supreme value of the cultural canon, are commensurate with the elevation of its position in the celestial arch.

For the collectivity the world of the cultural canon is as transpersonal as the world of the collective unconscious. The bond between the upper and lower semicircles, and between those two and the psyche of the group and of the individual, is unconscious.

The unity of life in this relatively self-contained sphere is secure and ordered as long as the higher corresponds to the lower. For in a balanced culture the collectivity and the individual integrated with the group are fed by the forces of the unconscious. In part, these forces flow into the personality through consciousness, which stands in direct communication with the constellations of the cultural canon in religion, art, custom, science, and daily life; in part, the unconscious is set in motion by the archetypes embodied in the cultural canon.

The diagram in Fig. 3 represents the disintegration of the canon, characteristic of our time and the century

cultural canon

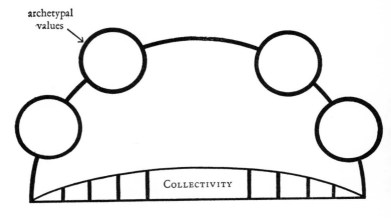

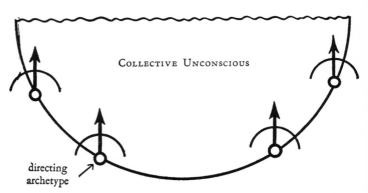

Fig. 2

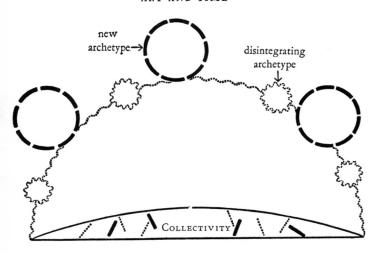

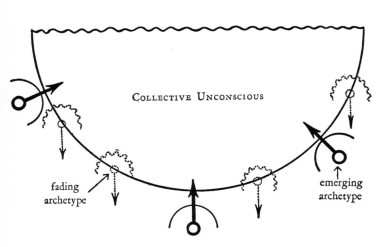

Fig. 3

or two preceding it. The equilibrium in the tension of the psychic field has been lost. In my figure the archetypes forming the canon seem to be fading out. The symbols corresponding to them disintegrate and the arch collapses because the underlying order has broken down. Just as a hive of termites or bees falls into chaos and panic as soon as the central power vested in the queen is destroyed, here too chaos and panic arise when the canonic order crumbles.

This chaos and the attendant atmosphere of doom are by no means diminished by the approach of other archetypes, which may actually have ushered in the collapse of the old cultural canon. Just as in antiquity and the Middle Ages, men today are afraid when stars fall, when comets move across the heavens, and when terrifying changes in the firmament and other signs announce the end of an epoch, which for the generation in question seems to be the end of the whole world.

For just as, archetypally, every New Year—or as in Aztec Mexico the beginning of every new end-of-year week [9]—is a perilous time of judgment and doom, so is the beginning of every new cultural epoch bound up with all that characterizes the end of an era. Only at rare intervals, when the clouds part in the dark sky of the crumbling canon, do a few individuals discern a new constellation, which already belongs to the new canon of transpersonal values and foreshadows its configuration.

We need not dwell at length on the trend of Western culture in the most recent centuries and particularly the

9. [Cf. Neumann, *The Great Mother*, p. 185, and Vaillant, *The Aztecs of Mexico*, pp. 195 f.—ED.]

last. This work of cultural critique has been done by great thinkers, particularly by Marx, Kierkegaard, Nietzsche, and Freud. The self-assurance and smugness of this age; its hypocrisy; its certainty of possessing everything that was good, true, noble, and beautiful; its indifference to the misery next door; the missionary and imperialist arrogance of this age, which thought it represented the peak and summit of humanity; its Victorianism, against a background of prostitution and French cancan—all this was an expression of the inner hollowness of values which had once held meaning and which mankind had built up at the cost of endless effort.

Since then, all these stage properties have rotted away; today the disintegration of our cultural canon is evident, and it is the general symptoms of this disintegration which characterize our time and its expression in art. It seems to me that on the whole this disintegration is similar to that which occurs in an individual when for some reason his individual canon, his conscious world of values, collapses.

The disappearance of the certainty and security once conferred by the cultural canon shows itself primarily in a sense of isolation, of forlornness, of homelessness and alienation, which has vastly increased in the course of the last hundred years. Probably never before in the history of literature or painting have there been so many isolated individuals. The concepts of school, tradition, and unity of style seem to have vanished. At a distance, of course, we can discover certain kinships; yet each individual seems to have felt the necessity of starting from the very beginning.

III

Consider, to mention only a few of the painters of the last sixty years, such figures as Cézanne, Van Gogh, Gauguin, Rousseau, Munch, Klee, Matisse, Chagall, Picasso—there has never been anything similar in history. Each of them is a world in himself, endeavoring alone to ward off the chaos that menaces him or to give it form, each with his own characteristic desperation. It is no accident that we hear so much today of the void and the forlornness of the individual. And the profound anxiety, the sense of insecurity, uprootedness, and world dissolution, at work in these painters also move modern composers and poets.

True, just as there is still a preanalytical psychology, there still exists an art that belongs to the day before yesterday. But the false innocence of this pseudo art, which strives to illuminate life with the light of stars that set long ago, is no less disquieting than the modern art that belongs to our time. To this day-before-yesterday's beauty the words of the *I Ching* apply: "But [the superior man] dare not decide controversial issues in this way [that is, according to beauty of form]." [10] And indeed today we are confronted with great and controversial questions.

Thus in our age, as never before, truth implies the courage to face chaos. In his *Dr. Faustus,* in which he embodies the profoundest insight into the character of our time, Thomas Mann says of Leverkühn's *Apocalypse,* that expression of modern despair: "The whole

10. *The I Ching, or Book of Changes,* Hexagram 22: *Pi* (Grace), p. 97. Also cf. Wilhelm, *Der Mensch und das Sein,* p. 211.

work is dominated by the paradox (if it is a paradox) that in it dissonance stands for the expression of everything lofty, solemn, pious, everything of the spirit; while consonance and firm tonality are reserved for the world of hell, in this context a world of banality and commonplace." [11]

When the world of security crumbles, man is inevitably devoured by *nigredo,* the blackness and chaos of the *prima materia,* and the two great archetypal figures of the Devil and the Terrible Mother dominate the world. The Devil is shadow, evil, depression, darkening of the light, harsh dissonance. Elsewhere I have discussed at greater length this incursion of the dark aspect into the Western world and, to the displeasure of those who like to see the world through rose-colored glasses, attempted to draw its ethical consequences.[12]

Consider the great line which begins with Goethe's *Faust* and the Romantic Doppelgänger literature: Melville's *Moby Dick,* Poe, Baudelaire, Trakl, Heym, Kubin, Kafka, and their heirs in modern crime fiction and films. Consider how the dark prophecies of misery, sickness, crime, and madness have been realized, how the black hordes of darkest mankind have shaken the world. Hell, *nigredo,* has been let loose and, as in the paintings of Bosch, peoples our reality. Those whom this blackness has almost blinded do not believe that nature is good, man noble, progress natural, or the godhead a good God.

This darkening brings with it dissonance; the "beautiful" is abandoned for the true, for so-called ugliness.

11. Tr. H. T. Lowe-Porter, p. 375.
12. My *Depth Psychology and a New Ethic.*

And the dissonance characteristic of the contemporary world has not only carried its dark, negative *content* into our consciousness but has concurrently brought about a general disintegration of form. Behind the archetype of Satan and the blackness surrounding him, at whose impact the crumbling world of the old cultural canon has collapsed, rises the devouring Terrible Great Mother, tearing and rending and bringing madness. And everywhere in modern art we see this dissolution in the breakdown and decay of form.

The libido would seem to have withdrawn from the once round and solidly modeled outside world and flowed inward. In painting, the world, formerly seen as real, has become one of appearance and illusion. This process began with the Impressionists, who abandoned the "illusory depth" of perspective, optical surface, objective color, and outward unity. Similarly in literature, the laws of composition have broken down. The line from Goethe to Dostoevski to Proust and Joyce is not a line of degeneration, but it does mark the increasingly conscious dissolution of style, human personality, and the unified work.

In Dostoevski's novels, for example, we have no longer a plastic individuality but a psychic movement which shatters all form, even that of the individual; what he essentially reveals is not any single man but the numinous powers of the inner world.

Even in such great portrayers of character as Balzac and Tolstoi we find an analogous dissolution of the plastic individual. A collective process, the group or the epoch, replaces the individual as the actual "hero." This

does not mean that the individual is no longer characterized as an individual or that there is no emphasis on
literary form. But the central character is a collective
entity, which is seen not only in sociological but in much
more universal terms: war, money, marriage, etc. The
novel has ceased to be purely personal and is peopled
with transpersonal powers. And where the family novel
does appear as such, its emphasis is on the passing generations, the changing times, and epochs and their decay.

Unity of time, place, and action; unity of character;
plasticity of the individual; the *Bildungsroman*—how
harmless and dated they all seem at a time when chaos
threatens to engulf us and every serious work of art must
directly or indirectly come to grips with this problem.
For even where the problem is formulated differently,
even where it assumes a philosophical or sociological, a
theological or psychological, coloration—if we consider it
as a whole, we perceive an immense anxiety and indeed
a clear consciousness of great danger. And this was true
long before our own epoch of world wars and atom
bombs.[13] The chaos was first discernible within; this

13. It is highly questionable whether we can derive all these
manifestations from the decay of our social structure. We can
equally well demonstrate the contrary, that the disintegration of
the cultural canon, originating in the unconscious, leads to the
collapse of the social structure. More significant than any typo-
logically determined overemphasis of inward or outward causality, in my opinion, is the realization that we have to do with an
integral psychic field embracing two worlds in which changes
occur simultaneously. Such prophecies regarding the future of
our culture as those of Heine and Nietzsche show that the disease
of the times can be diagnosed from within as well as from
without.

danger threatened from within; and perhaps more than any art before it, modern art is turned inward.

If we have abandoned outward unity, quasi-reality, it is in response to an overwhelming force from within us; the annihilation of everything that passed as good has brought with it the devastation of all that was held to be real. Outstandingly in Joyce this force from within is manifested as an erupting stream of language, as involuntary creation.

It is at this point that psychoanalysis and depth psychology, which are analogous phenomena from another part of our psychic field, invaded modern art as a whole —not merely literature; they have fructified its development in every sphere. The method of free association is an instrument for the discovery of unconscious contents and their movement, and it is also a destroyer of form and of conscious systematization, which now seem a fraud and façade, a figment of the "outside world," without inner truth.

In reality this incursion of the irrational into art was a legitimate expression of the time long before the Surrealists made a dogma of it. The surrender of conscious control is only a consequence of the disintegration of the cultural canon and of the values by which alone consciousness had oriented itself. And if the Surrealists made dreams, sickness, and madness the central content of art and tried to make their writing and painting flow directly from the unconscious, this was merely a late caricature of what was suffered by the great creative personalities, for they all stand under the sign of Orpheus, who was rent to pieces by the maenads. And in consequence the art which expresses our time seems to consist only of fragments, not of complete works. For the swarms of "little" artists the absence of canon imposed by the situation has itself become canon, and this is what gives rise to all our current "isms."

Here again the Great Men differ from the little. The great artists make conscious use of the situation, dissolving configured outward reality into a stream of feeling and action that, though coming from within, is nevertheless directed; this is equally true of Klee or Chagall, of Joyce or Thomas Mann. The lesser artists make a program of this principle; they amuse themselves and the world with the literary and artistic expression of their incontinence, with an exhibition of their private complexes. For example, Dali.

The modern painters of the last sixty years have been captured by a power which threatens to destroy them. These painters are not masters in the old sense, but victims, even when they dominate this situation. Because the form of the outside world has been shattered, an identifiable and learnable artistic technique has almost ceased to exist. All these artists suffer the demonic violence of the inward powers. Whether they are driven like Munch into solitude and sickness, like Van Gogh into the release of madness, like Gauguin to the distant isles of primitivism, or like Picasso into the amorphous world of inner transformation—their despair and the strain under which they work contrast sharply with the tranquillity of earlier artists, who felt that they were carrying on a tradition.

We find in Kubin and the early Klee the grotesque

distortion, the anxiety and distress, that come of inundation by the unconscious; we find it in Odilon Redon
and Ensor, in Lautrec and Munch. A sinister quality, a
fear of world catastrophe, are apparent not only in the
fractured lines of the paintings of Picasso and Braque
but equally in much modern sculpture, with its disorgan-
ized fragments of shattered bodies.

The dream world of Chirico and the spirit world of
Barlach are interrelated, just as they are related to Rim-
baud and Rilke, to *The Magic Mountain* despite its totally different configuration, and to Hesse's *Steppenwolf.*
Over them all stands anxiety, the incursion of *die andere
Seite* (the Other Side), which Kubin intuitively anticipated.

As our daytime world is devoured by the Terrible
Mother, torn to pieces in the bloody rituals that are our
wars, demonic, magical, and elemental irrationality in-
vades us. The stream of the libido flows inward, from
the crumbling canon into the unconscious, and activates
its latent images of past and future.

This is why the art of primitive peoples, of children,
and of the insane arouses so much interest today; everything is still in mixture and almost unarticulated. It is
almost impossible to render this phase of the world faith-
fully, because we are still in a formless state of creative
disintegration: protoplasm, mingling decay and new
birth—amorphous, atonal, disharmonious, primeval.

Blackness, *nigredo,* means the breakdown of distinc-
tions and forms, of all that is known and certain. When
the psychic libido of the individual drains off into the
darkness, he falls back into *prima materia,* into a chaos

in which the psychic state of origination, of *participation mystique,* is reactivated. And in modern art we find the same phenomenon. The dissolution of the outside world, of form and the individual, leads to a dehumanization of art.

The vital energy leaves the human form that was hitherto its highest embodiment and awakens extra-human and prehuman forms. The human figure that corresponds in a psychological sense to the personality centered in the ego and the system of consciousness is replaced by the anonymous vitality of the flowing un-conscious, of the creative force in nature and the psyche.

This process is evident in the landscapes of the Im-pressionists. The transformation begins with the outside world, which becomes psychic and gradually loses its objective character. Instead of painting a segment of the outside world, the artist paints for painting's sake, con-cerning himself only with the inherent modality of the picture, with color and form; the psychic symbol has re-placed the object. But through *participation mystique* this psychic symbol has a closer, more effective, and more inward contact with the segment of world to which it relates than a naturalistic, objective picture, dictated by consciousness and "made" with detachment.

We find in modern paintings a strange mixture, a unity of world and psyche, in which fragments of land-scapes, cubes, circles, forms, colors, parts of human fig-ures, organic and inorganic components, curves, tatters of dreams, memories, deconcretized objects, and con-cretized symbols seem to float in a strange continuum. We are reminded of the myth that, before the world was created with its familiar figures, fragments came into being, arms, heads, eyes, torsos, etc., without interconnection, which appeared only in a later birth.

Whether Picasso represents this world of the beginning or in his cubist efforts he opposes its chaos, whether in harmony with the life stream of color Chagall hovers lyrically over this world, or Klee, with the knowledge of an initiate, chisels out the secret counterpoint of its inner order, the driving force is in every case the *participation mystique,* the inner stream that follows its own laws, detached from the illusion of outward reality.

All this is deconcretized; and if corks and cookies, scraps of paper, or other articles are pasted on the picture, this quasi-concreteness only makes the spectral quality of the whole even more evident. Dynamics replaces composition, the energy of color and form replaces the illusion of outward reality, the amorphous replaces the conventional and matter of fact, and disintegration and the abyss banish comfort and "still life."

This deconcretization is also expressed in the two-dimensional trend of painting, which relinquishes the corporeality of world and body for a dynamic of form and color—a trend, by the way, which has its analogy in science, in both physics and psychology.

The human becomes demonic, things become human: a face dissolves into colors and forms, a blob of paint looks at us with a human eye. Everything shifts and leaps, now into empty banality, now into an abyss of cosmic suffering, now into a mystical transfiguration of color. Whip all this together and mix it with the unintelligible—isn't that just what life really looks like? But even if we recognize that this modern art is an authentic expression of our time, the question arises: Is it still art in the same sense as all previous art? And although those who first called it "degenerate art" were themselves degenerates, has our art not really gone astray?

But let us be careful! We are speaking of ourselves. If this art is degenerate, we too are degenerate, for innumerable individuals are suffering the same collapse of the cultural canon, the same alienation, the same loneliness—the rising blackness with its shadow and devouring dragon. The disintegration and dissonance of this art are our own; to understand them is to understand ourselves.

If the need for expression has its source in the intensity of the experience, how can modern man, whose world is menaced by chaos, do other than give creative form to this chaos? Only where chaos is overcome can what lies behind it emerge, and the seed of the fruit of chaos is perhaps more precious than the seed of any other fruit. Today there can be no hope for the future in any religion, art, or ethic that has not faced this threat of chaos.

That a new ethic is needed is neither a philosophical whim nor merely the product of an unfortunate disposition; it is a profound concern of our time.[14] Here the men of today and the men of yesterday must part company. Anyone whose ears do not burn, whose eyes do not cloud over, at the thought of the concentration camps, the crematoriums, the atomic explosions which make up our reality—at the dissonances of our music, the broken, tattered forms of our painting, the lament of Dr. Faustus

14. Cf. my *Depth Psychology and a New Ethic.*

—is free to crawl into the shelter of the safe old methods and rot. The rest of us must again taste the fruit of the tree of knowledge, which will redeem us from the paradise in which it is believed that man and the world are wholly good. It is true that we run the risk of choking on it. But there is no other way. We must acknowledge the evil, the blackness, the disintegration which cry to us so desperately from the art of our time, and whose presence it so desperately affirms.

Paradoxical as it may sound when formulated in theological terms, it seems today that we must redeem a bit of Satan. It is not without significance that I have never met any man for whom the idea of hell as eternal punishment, the idea of absolute damnation, was not utterly inconceivable. Hell no longer seems an inhuman, alien conception, for all of us are too close to this hell within us and outside us; all of us are consciously or unconsciously dominated by the numinous law of transformation, which leads to hell, and also through it and beyond it.

Again I must quote from *Dr. Faustus,* this time Frau Schweigestill's words, with which the tragedy ends: "Often he talked of eternal grace, the poor man, and I don't know if it will be enough. But an understanding heart, believe me, is enough for everything."

Let us understand these words correctly. They are not proud or arrogant; on the contrary they are desperately modest. We really do not know any longer whether grace is enough, precisely because we are as we are and are beginning to see ourselves as we are. But at a time of overwhelming crisis, the questionable nature of grace, or rather our knowledge that we are unworthy of grace, compels us to understand and love mankind, the fallible mankind that we ourselves are. Behind this abysmal crisis, the archetype of the Eternal Feminine as earth and as Sophia would seem to be discernible; it is no accident that these words are spoken by Frau Schweigestill, the mother. That is to say, it is precisely in chaos, in hell, that the New makes its appearance. Did not Kwanyin descend into hell rather than spend her time with the serene music makers in heaven?

Modern art, then, is not concerned with beauty, much less with aesthetic pleasure. Modern paintings are no museum pieces. Since they are not primarily the product of a directing consciousness, they can only be effective and fruitful when the beholder himself is in an adequate psychic situation—that is, not centered in his ego consciousness but turned toward his own unconscious, or at least open to it.

There is in modern art a psychic current which descends like a waterfall into the chasm of the unconscious, into a nonobjective, impersonal world. With their animism that brings to life the inner world and the realm of *participation mystique,* many of these works are charged with a demonic force that can suddenly leap out at the overwhelmed and terrified beholder at any time, in any place, and strike him like lightning, for modern art lives in a world between chaos and archetype; it is filled with plasmatic forces out of which such an archetype can suddenly be constellated.

Sometimes the powers themselves appear, as in the spectral, demonic world of Kubin, in Ensor's masks, and to a lesser degree in Dali. True, most modern artists deprecate realistic, objective representations of demonic forces, and indeed there are countless other ways of expressing the powers. They range from Barlach's picture of a world dominated by unseen forces to the plastic abstractions of Henry Moore and Picasso's abstract grotesque demonism.

Distortion, crookedness, and grotesque horror form an archetypal aspect of the demonic. If modern art is characterized by the disintegration of external reality and an activation of the transpersonal psychic world, it becomes understandable that the artist should feel a compulsion to depict the powers in their own realm—which is, of course, a psychic realm—and not as they appear, disguised, in nature. And in the art of primitives also, abstraction is often the form corresponding to the world of spirits and the dead.

As magnets order a field of iron filings, so do the archetypes order our psychic life; a similar process takes place in modern painting. Among primitive peoples the powers are projected into strange forms and symbols, and modern art has returned to this primordial phase of exorcism.

In Western culture the artist first set out to represent the world implied in the idea of the beautiful; he strove to concretize this transfigured vision, and later, with the emergence of the earth archetype, the ideal of the beautiful seemed to have been imprinted on life itself. The modern development, however, has been to shatter all these static, ontological conceptions. The powers become visible as pure dynamic, no longer incarnated in man and object.

He who has perceived the numinosum which destroys every canon, dissolves every fixed system, and reduces every form to relativity tends to see the godhead as an irrupting power, a lord of destruction who dances like Shiva himself over a collapsing world. And it is easy to misinterpret our world and its art in this sense—as annihilation. For all of us are still accustomed to believe in set images, in absolute ideas and values, to see the archetype only as eternal presence and not as formless dynamic, to forget the central commandment of the godhead, which is: "Thou shalt not make unto thyself any graven image."

But it is a total misunderstanding of our time and our art to regard their relation to chaos as purely negative. For all these artists have one thing in common: they have all experienced the creative truth that the spirit blows where it will; and even where they seem to be playing and leaving things to chance, it is not only because the perplexed ego has renounced all hope of knowledge but because they believe profoundly that in and behind chance a greater truth may be at work. Conscious renunciation of form is often falsely interpreted as inability to give form, as incompetence. Actually the breakdown of consciousness, carrying the artist backward to an all-embracing *participation* with the world, contains the constructive, creative elements of a new world vision.

The deflation of man makes for a sense of world and life far transcending the common bond which unites all men on earth. It is no accident that a human element appears so seldom at the center of the modern mandala, and so frequently a flower, a star, a spring, a light, an eye, or the void itself. The center of gravity has shifted from consciousness toward the creative matrix where something new is in preparation.

This shift is perhaps most evident in Chagall's paintings, which reflect most clearly the synthetic force of the soul's emotional reality. The luminous power of the inward colors, an inward movement guided by a stream of symbols, produces paintings which are an authentic metaphor for the inward life of the psyche. And beyond all chaos, yet profoundly bound up with it, there arises a new kind of psychic beauty, psychic movement, and irrational unity, whose flowerlike growth—otherwise found only in Klee, and here in a different form—is rooted in the profoundest and most secret depths of the soul.

Our art contains as many revelations of the archetype as of chaos. Only the simplest form of this reawakened archetypal world is reflected among the neoprimitives, whether like Gauguin they seek archaic form or like Rousseau represent the archetypes in naïve splendor: the desert, the forest primeval, the Great Mother as snake charmer, the battle in the jungle, or, contrasting with all this, the *petit bourgeois* world, the nosegay, etc.

An animistic, pantheistic sense of a world animated by the archetypes is revealed in the autonomous dynamic of natural form, as in Cézanne, the cubists, and modern plastic art. Not only in Van Gogh and Munch, but actually in all moderns, whether they paint portraits, landscapes, or abstractions, this autonomous dynamic creates psychic landscapes whose mood, emotion, color—the inner music of primal feeling, line and form, and the primal constellations of form and color—are the authentic expression of the powers. These powers everywhere, in wind and cube, in the ugly and absurd, as well as in stone or stream—and ultimately in the human as well—are manifested as movement, never as given and fixed things.

For the art of our time inclines toward a radical spiritualism, a solemnization of the secret transpersonal and suprapersonal forces of life and death, which surge up from within to compensate for the materialism dominating the outward picture of our times, a materialism conditioned by the rise of the earth archetype during the Renaissance.

Thus it is a great misunderstanding to characterize this art as intellectual—for only its hangers-on are intellectual—and to underestimate its religious and, in the true sense of the word, metaphysical impetus. The anonymous creative drive itself is the essential reality of a human art independent of any external world. Our art, like our times, is characterized by the old Chinese saying quoted by Richard Wilhelm: "The heavens battle with the creatures in the sign of the Creative." [15]

In compensation for the decay of our cultural canon and our permanent values, both the individual and the group are experiencing an awakening of the collective unconscious. Its inward, psychic expression is modern art, but it is also outwardly discernible in the flood of

15. Wilhelm, *Der Mensch und das Sein*, p. 234.

religious, spiritual, and artistic forms that are erupting from the collective unconscious into Western consciousness.

The art of diverse epochs and religion, peoples and cultures, tends to merge in our modern experience. In the symbols of their worshipers' rapture the gods of all times confront us, and we stand overwhelmed by this inward pantheon of mankind. Its expression is the world's art, that prodigious net of numinous creation in which man is captured, although he himself has brought it forth.

The dignity of man now appears to us in his creative power, whether in the modern or the Indian, in the medieval Christian or the Bushman. All together are the creators of a higher reality, of a transpersonal existence, whose emanation, transcending times and cultures, shows man in his creative reality and spurs him toward it.

The revelation of the numinosum speaks out of every creative man regardless of his cultural level, for there are different aspects of the transpersonal, which leads one individual to a religious calling, another to art, still another to a scientific or an ethical vocation. The fraternity of *all* those who have been seized by the numinosum is one of the great human phenomena we are beginning to perceive in this era which, more than any other before it, is gaining an awareness of the immensity of man's works.

The religions of the world, the saviors of the world, the revolutionaries, the prophets, and not least the artists of the world—all these great figures and what they have created form for us a single whole. We all—and not just individuals among us—are beginning not to free ourselves from our personal determinants, for that is impossible, but to see them in perspective. The African medicine man and the Siberian shaman assume for us the same human dignity as Moses and the Buddha; an Aztec fresco takes its place beside a Chinese landscape and an Egyptian sculpture, the Upanishads beside the Bible and the Book of Changes.

At the center of each culture and time stand different numinous—or, as we say, archetypal—powers, but all are eternal, and all touch upon the eternal existence of man and the world. Whether it be Egypt's striving for permanence, Mexico's primitive terror, the human radiance and clarity of Greece; whether it be the faith of the Psalmist, the transfigured suffering of Jesus or the Buddha withdrawing into the infinite, the power of death in Shiva, Rembrandt's light, the emptiness of an Islamic mosque, the flowering earth of the Renaissance, the flaming earth of Van Gogh, or the dark earth of the African demons—all bear witness to the timelessness of man's seizure by the numinosum.

For the source of the creative drive is not nature, not the collective, not a definite cultural canon, but something which moves through generations and peoples, epochs and individuals, which calls the individual with the rigor of an absolute; and whoever he may be, and wherever he may be, it compels him to travel the road of Abraham, to leave the land of his birth, his mother, and the house of his father, and seek out the land to which the godhead leads him.

129

In our time two forms of integration appear side by side, an outward and an inward, a collective and an individual. Much as they may seem to differ, they are essentially related. The one is the integration incumbent upon our culture, an integration with world culture and all its contents. Inundation by the world's collective contents leads first to chaos—in the individual as in the group as a whole. How can the individual, how can our culture, integrate Christianity and antiquity, China and India, the primitive and the modern, the prophet and the atomic physicist, into *one* humanity? Yet that is just what the individual and our culture must do. Though wars rage and peoples exterminate one another in our atavistic world, the reality living within us tends, whether we know it or not, whether we wish to admit it or not, toward a universal humanism. But there is an inward process of integration which compensates for the outward one; this is individuation. This inner integration does not consist merely in the integration of the individual's personal unconscious; when the collective unconscious emerges, the individual must inwardly come to grips with the very same powers whose integration and assimilation as world culture are his outward tasks.

Our conception of man is beginning to change. Up to now we saw him chiefly in a historical or horizontal perspective, embedded in his group, his time, and his cultural canon, and determined by his position in the world —that is, in his particular epoch. There is truth in this vision, no doubt, but today we are beginning to see man in a new perspective—vertically—in his relation to the absolute.

The roots of every man's personality extend beyond the historical area of his factual existence into the world of the numinosum. And if we follow the course of these roots, we pass through every stratum of history and prehistory. We encounter within ourselves the savage with his masks and rites; within ourselves we find the roots of our own culture, but we also find the meditation of Asia and the magical world of the Stone Age medicine man. The challenge of this transpersonal world of powers must be met by modern man, despite his characteristic sense of inadequacy.

We must face our own problems and our own imperfections; and at the same time we must integrate a superabundant outward and inward world that is shaped by no canon. This is the conflict which torments modern man, the modern era, and modern art.

This integration of chaos, however, is not possible in any single act or constellation; the individuation it requires is a process of growth, embracing the transformations of a whole lifetime; during such a process each individual's capacity for resolving conflict is repeatedly strained to the utmost. This perhaps is why the careers of the great artists of our time are all, in greater or lesser degree, calvaries. The task of integration facing the great artist today can no longer be performed in a single work, but more than ever before requires a unity of life and work. Van Gogh's pictures cease in this sense to be individual paintings; they are a storm of painting bound up with his life, and each picture is only a part of it. But often it has even ceased to be the painter's intention—if we can speak here of intention—to achieve a complete statement in any one picture; his orientation is toward the work as a whole, which is meant to express a reality that transcends painting.

All modern artists—in contrast to the fulfilled artists of normal times—have the sacred enthusiasm of which the *I Ching* says: "Thunder comes resounding out of the earth: the image of enthusiasm," and "Devotion to movement: this is enthusiasm." [16]

Whether we consider Picasso, with his single-minded devotion to a great creative impulse—whose work represents a significant reality only when taken as a whole, each part being problematic, questionable, and incomplete; or Rilke, whose development leads from delicate sound arrangements through the catastrophe of ten years' silence to the gigantic dome of the *Duino Elegies;* or the even-paced building of Thomas Mann's work, increasingly preoccupied with what is evil, diseased, and archaic in man, which he (who, more than any other artist of our time, has achieved the unity of life and work that is individuation) uniquely integrated; when we consider the tragic frenzy of Van Gogh or the mysterious transformation of Klee—all of them belong to us; they are we, or rather we are fragments of them all.

We know that the core of the neuroses of our time is the religious problem or, stated in more universal terms, the search for the self. In this sense neuroses, like the mass phenomena resulting from this situation, are a kind of sacred disease. Our whole epoch is full of it, but behind it stands the power of a numinous center, which seems to direct not only the normal development of the

16. Vol. I, p. 71; Vol. II, p. 105.

individual but his psychic crises and transformations as well—not only the disease but also its cure, both in the individual and in the collective.

This centroversion has great consequences in the great and small consequences in the small. However, our whole art, which may be called neurotic in its rapture and "sacred" in its neurosis, is unconsciously or—in its highest summits—consciously directed by this central force. And so it is with each one of us.

Just as the psychic totality of the individual takes form around a mysterious center, the mandala of modern art, in all its vast diversity, unfolds around a mysterious center, which as chaos and blackness, as numinosum and as change, is pregnant with a new doom, but also with a new world. In the *Duino Elegies* Rilke wrote:

> For Beauty's nothing
> but beginning of Terror we're still just able to bear,
> and why we adore it so is because it serenely
> disdains to destroy us.[17]

More than to any other beauty in art, these words apply to the terrible beauty of modern art, which itself denies that it is beauty. Never before was the beautiful so close to the terrible. The masters of Zen Buddhism often twisted their disciples' noses or struck them in the face in order to bring them illumination by thrusting them back on themselves. Similarly, our time and our destiny, and often our art as well, strike us in the face, perhaps also in order to fling us into the void of the center, which is the center of transformation and birth.

17. Tr. Leishman and Spender, p. 25.

For despite all the despair and darkness which are still more evident in us and our art than the secret forces of the new birth and the new synthesis, we must not forget that no epoch, amid the greatest danger to its existence, has shown so much readiness to burst the narrow limits of its horizon and open itself to the great power which is striving to rise out of the unknown, here and everywhere in the world. Menaced as we are by our own atom bombs, every act of destruction will be answered by a rebuilding, in which the unity of everything human will be affirmed more strongly than ever.

This is surely no prophecy; it is the reality of the road which we travel, or rather which we are compelled to travel. Upon this road the horizons are changing in a way we ourselves scarcely realize, and we along with them are moving toward the New, all of us, on this side and that side of the iron curtains that divide us today.

Let us not forget that, despite all the darkness and danger, the man of our time, like the art that belongs to him, is a great fulfillment and a still greater hope.

# III

## NOTE ON MARC CHAGALL

Marc Chagall. The strange painter from Vitebsk is generally regarded as a Romantic, a painter of folklore. Some stress his "childlike" or primitive quality, others the idyllic aspect of his youth in a small town, or his Jewish milieu. But all these interpretations miss the essential.

He is not a great painter of the kind whose gradual growth takes in greater and greater areas of the outward or inner world. Nor is he a painter of upheaval like Van Gogh, who passionately experienced the nascent modern world in every cypress tree of Provence. But he is unique in the depth of feeling that carried him through the surface manifestations of his personalistic existence to the fundamental symbols of the world, the foundation underlying all personal existence.

His pictures have been called poems, they have been called dream images, implying that the intention of his painting extended to a plane removed from all painting —even that of our day. Perhaps only the Surrealists, who for this reason called Chagall the first Surrealist, shared his intention, which might in a certain sense be called a lack of intention. But—and this is the very crux of the matter—Chagall is no Surrealist working with the blind unconsciousness of Freudian free association. A profound, but by no means unformed, reality makes itself felt in his work. The dream law of his paintings flows from a unity of feeling, reflected not only in the intrinsic color development but also in the relationship between the symbols that order themselves round the symbolic center of the picture. These symbolic centers of Chagall's pictures are unquestionably spontaneous products of his unconscious, and not constructions of his ego. The consciousness that executes his painting follows the mood and inspiration of the unconscious. The unity and force of conviction in his pictures are an expression of the obedience with which he accepts the intention of his unconscious. Like a medium, undisturbed by the impressions and influences of the world around him, he follows the inner voice that speaks to him in symbols.

Here we touch on a central Jewish paradox in Chagall: a prophecy in which the godhead does not, as from time immemorial, speak in words, but in mystery and image—an unmistakable sign of the upheaval that has taken place in the Jewish soul.

Language, and the language of prophetic religion more than any other, is indeed rooted in the unconscious, with its stream of images; but Judaism and Jewish prophecy were formed by the ethical accent of a consciousness which derived its own central force from its analogy with the central power of the One God. The imperative guidance of this prophetic will so sharpened the intention of the unconscious forces that stood behind, heated it to so white a glow, that the images lost their colors; the variegated flowers of psychic life were turned to ashes.

But in Chagall for the first time something originating in the very same psychic stratum from which Jewish prophecy drew its power speaks in images and colors. In the new historical situation of a Jewish people transformed through the central depth of its unconscious, prophecy speaks a new language and utters new contents—the beginning of a new Jewish message to the world. The soul of Jewry, compressed by necessity into the shell of isolation, makes itself free, sinks its roots deep into the earth, and manifests itself in a first new flower.

At first glance there seems to be nothing very impressive about Chagall's Jewish provincialism. Folklore, the village idyll, the Jewish small town with its petty bourgeoisie, childhood memories—childhood memories over and over again. Who cares about this Jewish town, about all these relatives and bridal couples, these eccentrics and fiddlers, these festivals and customs, sabbath candles and cows, these scrolls of the Torah and village fences? Childhood—that is the milieu from which Chagall never escaped and to which he returns over and over again, regardless of Paris and Europe, of world wars and revolutions. All this may be lovable and touching, unless one prefers to call it sickly and sentimental. Is this all? one is justified in asking. What is all the fuss about? Is all this not a mere variant of modern primitivism, only a kind of colorful, romantic popular art? Chagall would give no answer, probably he would know no answer; he would only smile and keep on painting his colorful world, the same little houses, the same childhood memories, the same colored fragments of his early world: cows and fiddles, Jews and donkeys, candelabra and brides. But in the midst of it there are angels and moons, blazing fires, and the eye of God in the village. For what is childhood but the time of great events; the time in which the great figures are close at hand and look out from behind the corner of the house next door; the time in which the deepest symbols of the soul are everyday realities, and the world is still radiant with its innermost depth? This childhood reaches back to the earliest prehistory and embraces Abraham's angels as tenderly as the neighbor's ass; it experiences the wedding and the meeting between bride and bridegroom with the same joy and the same radiant color as the spring and the moonlit nights of first love. In this childhood there is as yet no separation between personal and suprapersonal, near and far, inward soul and outward world; the life stream flows undivided, joining godhead and man, animal and world, in the glow and color of the nearby. This simultaneity of inside and outside, which perceives the world in the soul and the soul in the world; this simultaneity of past and future, which experiences the promise of the future in the remote past and the guilt of the ages in the anguish of the present—this is the reality of Chagall's childhood, and the eternal presence of the primordial images lives in his memory of Vitebsk.

For this reason there is no above and below in his paintings, no rigid, inanimate thing, nor any dividing line between man and animal, the human and the divine. In the ecstasy of love man still wears the ass's head of his animal nature and the angel's countenance shines amid calamity and doom. All Chagall's pictures are permeated by the soulful divine light—unbroken by the prism of the understanding—which in childhood fills the whole world; all reality becomes a symbol; every bit of the world is transformed into a divine mystery.

Presumably Chagall "knows" nothing of what befalls him in his pictures, but the pictures themselves know and bear witness to their knowledge. There is the beloved, over and over again, in endless transformations, as soul, as angel, and as the inspiring power of the feminine. In one painting the artist—assuredly without knowledge of the ass Lucius, the unregenerate lower man in Apuleius' romance—bears an ass's head as he stands at his easel and the feminine soul figure guides his eyes upward; in another picture it is the angel himself who holds his palette, or else the figure of the anima, the soul, may peer out of the easel. In every case he expresses the unconscious knowledge that his hand is guided and that an earthly creature is receiving inspiration and guidance from an unearthly, suprapersonal force. In all these visions the masculine is dull, bestial, earth-bound, while the feminine blooms in all the colors of a transfigured, unearthly radiance.

This emphasis on the feminine reflects something essentially new in the outlook of Jewish mankind, which hitherto with its ethic and spirit seemed so fundamentally patriarchal that the feminine, repressed and almost despised, could speak to it only through subterranean channels. In Chagall it is not only the compensating contrary aspect that breaks through, as in the mystical undercurrents of Jewish cultural history; rather, he is the prophet of a nascent new reality, of an upheaval from out of the depths. It is this alone that justifies us in speaking of Chagall's prophetic mission.

The feminine soul figure that fills Chagall's world reaches out beyond his own personal sphere and indeed exceeds the limits of any purely Jewish contemporary constellation; for the circle whose center it forms is the primordial circle of archetypal symbols, such symbols as night or moon, bride or angel, loving one or mother. But it is striking, and characteristic for the situation of the modern man and the Jew, that the mother with child seldom occupies the center of these pictures. The Madonnalike mother with child who appears in Chagall's paintings has always played a significant role in Jewish life as the collectively regenerating emotional force of the feminine. But she has always remained a symbol of collective forces, and has never become truly incarnated as an individual feminine power in life, or as a feminine force deep within the psyche of the Jewish man. But the essential is the individual incarnation of the soulful and feminine in man, and this is how the feminine appears in Chagall and dominates his pictures: as a configuration of the magical and fascinating, inspiring and ecstatic soul that transforms the world with the starfall of its colors.

For this reason the center of his work is the relation of the masculine to this type of the feminine; and for this reason it is in the lovers that the secret reality of the world flowers mysteriously over and over again. Cha-

gall's Vitebsk and likewise his Paris are full of this bride
and bridegroom, whom he never wearies of painting; in
them live the darkness of nocturnal drives and the
golden light of the soul's ecstasy. The ass of the body
may stagger, it may rise on wings to higher realms; in
the form of a gigantic, glowing red angel it may hold
the chalice with the sacred wine of drunkenness; and
yet again the moon may stand so close to the lovers that
the distant bridge, like the rim of reality, marks the
limit of the transfiguration in which lovers, angels, and
flowers hold out their hands to one another, in which
the interweaving of drive and soul, the human and the
divine, of color and light, is always the one encounter,
which lives behind all the rest, the meeting of the bridegroom with the bride. But this is the encounter of the
transcendent God with his feminine immanence; it is
the encounter of *keter* and *Shekinah,* of God and soul,
of man and world, which takes place in the inner reality
of every living couple.

Here the cabalistic and Hasidic symbolism of Jewish
mysticism become the reality of a man drunk with love,
whose rich palette bears witness that creative man is
made in God's image, and in whose pictures of human
life in the world the creation begins forever anew.

The lovers are God's seal on the world, the seal in
which his bond with the reality of man is confirmed like
a new rainbow of promise. For despite all the terror, despite all the pogroms and crucifixions, despite all the
fires and wars, this earthly life is the consolation of the
godhead itself, if it is taken as the symbol that it is.

The white cow lying beside the Jew wrapped in the

tallith of his loneliness is the appeasement of the maternal world; and in the nocturnal village whose poor little houses stand low and crooked between the fields and fences, there gleams the gigantic, wide-open eye of God (Pl. VII). It watches us always, always it sees the world and us in it and itself; and everywhere it is the center of reality that becomes visible in the stillness as God's presence. Perhaps the woman milking the blue cow beneath the moon sees this eye less than she sees the chickens and the houses; but nonetheless it dominates the nighttime world and opens wherever the creature comes to himself.

But it is chiefly at night and under the moon, when the inwardness speaks and the world of the secret is unsealed, that the world comes to itself. And that is why the night is the time of ecstasy, when the soul's firebird in the form of a flaming rooster abducts the feminine and the music of lovers refashions the world in the perfect original unity from which it sprang in the beginning.

Yet this glowing interior world of Chagall—in which things occupy not their earthly place but the place they hold in the soul, the place assigned them by the creation that is even now in progress—this world is by no means an airy figment. Nor is it the world of miracles and magic spells, in which the Jewish mankind that draws Messianic time down to earth in prayer flies in ecstatic concentration over the historical time of reality. Rather, it is an earthly, real world of the soul, whose nocturnal roots reach deeper than the roots of a merely earthly life, down to the primordial stream of the images, which waters every living existence.

In Chagall's symbol world, the Jewish and the Christian, the individual and collective, primitive paganism and complex modernism, are fused into an indissoluble unity. The persecuted, massacred Jew with the phylacteries hangs as Christ on the Cross of suffering, and the cart, filled with all those terrified fugitives whose home is going up in flames, drives past the figure of the crucified one, who joins their suffering with his; for sacrifice and suffering are everywhere, and crucified mankind hangs everywhere from the Cross of the son of God. But side by side with this there is the pagan vitality of the animals; ram and ass become Panlike figures of the primordial pagan era, in which the angelic cuts across the divine. For nature is life with all its direct fullness of color and all its tragic depth, manifested in drives and instincts and in the wild drunkenness of ecstasy. Drunken knowledge pours from the red luminous wine and from the woman's white body no less than from the crucifix and the scroll of the Torah, and the desperate mixture of higher and lower in human nature becomes a mysterious coincidence of opposites in the one center of life.

Here past and future, higher and lower, fuse into a dreamlike reality; as in Chagall's enchanted forest, outside and inside appear as mirror worlds, reflecting a third world that hides its true reality behind them and in them.

This reality is just as much alive in the Jew at prayer and the rabbi as in the miserable servant girl and the drunkard, the rooster and the weary little horse. The transfiguration of sensuality in the nude lovers is the blazing fiery rooster, whose ecstatic arc cuts through the night; and the lovers in the boat or under the bridge glow like the sabbath candles or the red sun of the wedding.

All these planes of God's hidden world become visible in Chagall's pictures; they appear in the natural, that is, divine, intermixture that determines the world of the soul: natural thing and symbol; specter and reality; harlequinade of life and lovers' magic; naked drive and religious ecstasy; pillaging soldiers and the silver, fish-tailed dancer of the soul; trumpets of judgment and the endless train of mothers with child, of Marys on the flight to Egypt; the apocalyptic end of the world and the October Revolution; scrolls of the Torah, crucifixes, candelabra, cackling hens, ecstatic asses, and radiant violins whose music hovers between heaven and earth. And over and over again the moon.

The godhead speaks in colors and symbols. They are the core of the world of feeling and truth, a truth of the heart, the subterranean dream reality which, like a net of colored veins, runs through existence. For the "real world" is only a feeble illusion that forces itself on the sober; only the drunken eye of the creative man can see the authentic world of images. One of Chagall's paintings bears the motto that for him embodies the secret of all authentic life or knowledge of God: *Devenir flamme rouge et chaude*. Only the flame, the passionate devotion that summons up the profound powers of the psychic in man and makes them flow, can reveal the secret of the world and its divine heart.

But all this should not be taken in a pantheistic sense; it is not a universal statement about the presence of the

144

godhead. Close as Chagall's work is to Jewish mysticism and to symbols such as *hitlahavut* (passionate devotion) and *dveikut* (adhesion to the divine), it must not be reduced to these narrow limits. The depth and scope of a revelation correspond to the depth and scope of the psychic intention for which it is revealed, for which the world as a whole is first manifested as a creative secret. And we find similar intentions and unconscious insights throughout modern painting and modern art in general, and in modern man wherever he attains to the heart of actuality. For the reaction against the mechanized and soulless forces, in man as well as the machine, against the soulless mechanization that threatens to stifle the world, is the rebellion of the soul and the inward plunge of modern mankind.

The irruption and descent of the soul into Jewish mankind—this event with which Chagall is possessed and which he proclaims—was long in preparation. Millennia were needed before the godhead could descend from the hard grandeur of the all-governing law, from the steep summit of Sinai, before it could make its way through the luminous spirit worlds of the cabalistic spheres and transcendent divine secrets to the warm earthly fervor of Hasidic mysticism.

With the Diaspora the fenced-in Jewish community opened to the world, and this descent into the world, begun in exile, is at the same time—this, in any case, is the secret hope of Jewish destiny—the rise of the Jew's new psychic reality. This strange people, with its mixture of youth and age, primitivism and differentiation, prophetic fervor and worldly, world-building ethos, of extreme materialism and timeless spirituality—and Chagall is eminently an expression of all these traits—is engaged in a transformation. Regathered in the face of impending doom, the Jews are sowing once more the seeds assembled in centuries of exile. It is an age of degeneration and rot; the primordial world rises to the surface, the angels fall; but in all this the soul is reborn. Yet like all birth, this birth of the human soul occurs "inter urinas et faeces." The supreme values collapse, the candelabra totter, vainly the angels blow the shofar of judgment, and bearded Jews unroll the parchment scrolls of the Torah. Everything is carried downward by the fall of a world, and this catastrophe, this crucifixion, is enacted in a sea of blood, violence, pain, and tears. The crematoriums of the concentration camps and the mountains of corpses of the world wars are the stations in this catastrophe and this transformation. For the catastrophe is a rebirth.

The fate of Jewish mankind is also the fate of Europe, the fall of Vitebsk is also that of Paris, and the wandering Jew is the wandering of countless millions of uprooted men, of Christians and Jews, Nazis and Communists, Europeans and Chinese, of orphans and murderers. A migration of individuals, an endless flight from the extreme limits of Asia through Europe to America, an endless stream of transformation, whose depths are unfathomable and whose aim and direction seem impossible to determine. But from this chaos and catastrophe, the eternal rises up in unsuspected glory, the eternal that is age-old and then again utterly new. Not from outside but from inside and below shines the mys-

terious light of nature, the divine gloriole of the Shekinah, consoling and healing—the feminine secret of
transformation.

Chagall's aloofness from the events of the world is
anything but indifference to the happenings of his time.
Perhaps the pain-drenched colors of the dying villages
and homeless fugitives in Chagall's pictures mourn and
suffer more profoundly than Picasso's famous *Guernica*.
Chagall lacks monumentality because any rigid, monumental form is bound to dissolve in such a swirling
stream of emotion, because the pain is too great and its
immediacy hollows out all circumscribed form from
within. It is the dissolution of a world out of joint, a
world whose whole soil is shot through with volcanic
crevices; the norms collapse, floods of lava destroy the
existing order, but geysers of creativity spurt from the
tortured soil. For in this very dissolution a deeper plane
of reality is disclosed, yielding its secret to those who,
torn like the world itself, experience its primordial psychic source, which is also their own. The divine and the
human travel the same road, the world and man are not
a duality of one confronting the other; they are an inseparable unity. The moon rises in the soul of every individual, and the house in whose forehead the eye of the
godhead opens is you yourself.

Chagall's aloofness is that of the lover who looks toward the one unknown that gives him the certainty of
his own being-alive. It is the age-old covenant of Jew
and man with the God who, shorn of all limits, not only
offers his succor, but sacrifices himself to every nation
and every individual. In each man Sinai burns, each man

is crucified; but each man is also the whole of creation and the son of God.

Like the break-through of the soul in modern man in general, Chagall's break-through is not so much an act as a suffering of the naked truth concerning the man to whom our epoch does something that it does to every man who truly lives in it. Nothing human remains except for what is divine. Chagall's aloofness is the experience of a man to whom the divine-human world has opened, because the earthly-human is so drenched in the horror and suffering of transformation that his feeling can only remain alive if he keeps a perpetual hold on the heart of existence.

# IV

## CREATIVE MAN
## AND TRANSFORMATION

Once again I have been asked to discuss a subject so boundless that I cannot dispel a feeling of inadequacy. Creative transformation: each of these two words embraces a mysterious, unknown world. Transformation alone—the whole work of C. G. Jung, from his early *Wandlungen und Symbole der Libido* [1] to *Psychology and Alchemy* and the most recent work on the transformation symbolism of the Mass, is an untiring attempt to encompass the meaning of this word.

And when we turn to the adjective "creative," how can we help being assailed by a sense of utter hopelessness? On the one hand the image of the creative God

1. [This work, first published in 1912, appeared in Beatrice Hinkle's English translation in 1916 as *Psychology of the Unconscious*. The 4th Swiss edn., much revised, was published in 1952 as *Symbole der Wandlung;* translated as *Symbols of Transformation,* 1956, vol. 5 of the Collected Works. *Psychology and Alchemy:* its chief contents were first published in the *Eranos-Jahrbücher 1935* and *1936,* and it appeared as vol. 12 of the Collected Works in 1953. "Transformation Symbolism in the Mass": first published in the *Eranos-Jahrbuch 1941* and translated in *Psychology and Religion: West and East,* vol. 11 of the Collected Works, 1958.—Ed.]

and of creation; on the other the image of the Creative with its six masculine lines, which, standing at the beginning of the Book of Changes, lends emphasis to the primordial connection between transformation and creation. But between these two great images of the world-creating God on the one hand and of the self-transforming divine world on the other, there emerges the human creative world, the world of culture and creativeness, which constitutes man as man and makes his life in the world worth living.

How infinitely vast is the realm evoked by the word transformation; it embraces every change, every strengthening and slackening, every broadening and narrowing, every development, every change of attitude, and every conversion. Every sickness and every recovery are related to the term transformation; the reorientation of consciousness and the mystical loss of consciousness in ecstasy are a transformation. Even the normalization and adaptation of a neurotic individual to a given cultural environment appear to one observer as a transformation of the personality, while another diagnoses an experience that makes over the whole personality as sickness and disintegration of the personality. Each of the many religious, psychological, and political trends interprets transformation in a different way. And when we consider how limited and relative all of these points of view are, where is the psychologist going to find criteria that will enable him to say something about transformation pure and simple, not to mention creative transformation?

What we encounter most often are partial changes, partial transformations of the personality, and particularly of consciousness. Such partial transformations are by no means unimportant. The development of the ego and consciousness, the centroversion of consciousness in the middle of which the ego complex finds itself, the differentiation and specialization of consciousness, its orientation in the world and adaptation to it, its amplification by change of contents and assimilation of new contents—all these processes of normal development are highly significant processes of transformation. Down through the ages the development of man from child to adult, from primitive to differentiated culture, has been bound up with decisive transformations of consciousness.

Let us not forget that it is less than a hundred years since modern man ceased to regard the transformations of consciousness, i.e., of the partial personality, as almost all that mattered. Even since depth psychology has begun to reshape the outlook of modern man in a way that would have been inconceivable only a short time ago, the education of the individuals who make up the nations is directed almost entirely toward transformations of consciousness and conscious attitudes—or else transformation is held to be altogether unnecessary. Yet the experience of depth psychology has taught us that unless changes in consciousness go hand in hand with a change in the unconscious components of the personality, they do not amount to much. A purely intellectual orientation can, to be sure, bring about significant changes in consciousness, but for the most part such changes are restricted to the limited zone of consciousness. Whereas partial changes in the personal unconscious, in the "complexes," always influence consciousness at the same time, and changes effected through the archetypes of the collective unconscious almost always seize upon the whole personality.

Most striking are those transformations which violently assail an ego-centered and seemingly airtight consciousness, i.e., transformations characterized by more or less sudden "irruptions" of the unconscious into consciousness. The irruptive character is experienced with particular force in a culture based on ego stability and a systematized consciousness; for in a primitive culture, open to the unconscious, or in a culture whose rituals provide a bond with the archetypal powers, men are prepared for the irruption. And the irruption is less violent because the tension between consciousness and the unconscious is not so great.

In a culture where the psychic systems are separated, the ego experiences such irruptions primarily as "alien," as an outside force that "violates" it, and this feeling is partly justified. For chiefly where a pathological development or constitution has loosened the personality and made it permeable, where the ego has not acquired the necessary stability and the systematization of consciousness is incomplete, the chaotic stratum of repressed emotional charge rises up overpoweringly from the collective unconscious and attacks the weakest spot, which is the "irruptive personality."

But the psychological disorders having the character of alien invasion include also the irruptions provoked by a disturbance of the biological foundation of the psyche, which may be caused by organic disease, i.e., infections, by hunger, thirst, exhaustion, intoxicants, or medicines.

Related to these are the transformations known to us from the phenomenon of sudden conversion or illumination. But here the suddenness and strangeness of the irruption apply only to the affected ego and consciousness, not to the total personality. Usually the irruption into consciousness is only the culmination of a development that had long been maturing in the unconscious stratum of the personality; the irruption represents only the "bursting point" of a transformative process that has long been present but has not previously been perceptible to the ego.[2] For this reason such irruptions are not to be regarded as "alien" from the point of view of the total personality. But even the possession that accompanies an "achievement" or a creative process can take the form of psychic "irruption."

Yet psychic transformation and normalcy by no means stand in a fundamental opposition to one another. The phases of normal biophysical development—childhood, puberty, middle life, climacterium—are always transformative phases, subjectively critical in the life of the personality.

The normal development is characterized by a number of transformations that archetypal dominants help to guide. But here again it is difficult to distinguish the personal and individual from the archetypal, for in every ontogenesis the archetype crystallizes in and through the personal and individual; thus, for example, we inevitably experience the ages of man also as individual biography. Every childhood is both "childhood as such" and *my* own childhood. All these phases of

2. William James, *The Varieties of Religious Experience.*

transformation are common to the species and are at the same time unique, individual destiny. They represent natural transformations that should be understood in a total sense, i.e., biologically as well as sociologically. As total transformations they embrace the whole personality, consciousness as well as the unconscious, the relation between the two as well as the relation of the personality to the world and the human environment. The intensity and scope of these natural stages of transformation vary in the human sphere; but almost always childhood, love, maturity, old age, the expectation of death, are experienced and interpreted as crises, irruptions, catastrophes, and rebirths. That is why human culture set rituals in these places, rituals in which and through which the merely natural aspect of the developmental phase is raised to an awareness of psychic transformation.[3] In other words, the knowledge that man undergoes transformations, and that the world transforms itself with him and for him, is an element of every human culture.

Religion and ritual, festival and custom, initiation and experience of destiny, form a whole; they blind the individual to the culture of the collectivity just as they attach the life of the collectivity to the partial experience of the individual. The fact that the festivals and rites of transformation are almost always brought into consonance with the division of the year shows that the transformations of human development are experienced as one with the transformations of the natural world. In other words, the nature symbolism of the phenomena of

3. See my "Zur psychologischen Bedeutung des Ritus."

psychic transformation is experienced not only in itself but also as an authentic identity of inside and outside: new consciousness, birth of the light, and winter solstice are one. The same is true of resurrection, rebirth, and spring; of introversion, descent into hell or Hades, and autumn; of death, west, and evening; or of victory, east, and morning.

In all these cases the natural transformation of the developmental phase was enhanced and made conscious by culture, either for all the members of a culture or, as in the secret societies and mysteries, for certain individuals. And this means that in human culture man not only experiences himself as one who is transformed and should be transformed, but, in addition, that this specifically human transformation is felt to be something that is not merely natural. In primitive cultures, as we know, man "must" be initiated. What counts is not his age, not the transformation ordained by nature, but the initiatory transformation ordained by the collectivity; a higher process of transformation, transcending nature —a traditional, that is, specifically human, process—is exacted of him. In this process the spiritual side of the collectivity, the archetypal world as related to the cultural canon of the time, is conjured up, experienced, and solemnized as the creative source of collective and individual existence. This may be accomplished by means of mysteries or sacraments or in other ways; but in every case the fundamental phenomenon, common no doubt to all mankind, is a transformation that is induced by the cultural collectivity and prepares the individual for life in the collectivity. And there can be no doubt that these rites of transformation, which emphasize and enhance the phases of nature, are regenerative both in purpose and effect.

Although in our time this cultural sublimation of the natural transformations has been virtually lost, the natural curative power of the unconscious has been very largely preserved in the healthy, normal man. Not only is he guided through the phases of life—though less so than primitive man—by his phylogenic development, but moreover his whole life is molded by the compensatory action of the psyche with its tendency toward wholeness.

We have said that biopsychic transformation always embraces the whole of the personality, while possession by a personal complex, an emotional content, leads only to a partial transformation that overpowers consciousness and its center, the ego. Here one might be inclined to distinguish the complexes of the personal unconscious as negative from the creatively archetypal contents of the collective unconscious. But often in the healthy, creative man, as well as in the sufferer from mental disorder, the emotional complexes of the personal unconscious can only be separated very incompletely from the archetypal contents that stand behind them.

All psychoanalytic theories permit us to connect a possessed consciousness with a complex of the personal unconscious and reduce this complex to a feeling of inferiority, a mother fixation, an anxiety constellation, etc. But the problem must be put differently if the complex releases an achievement. Wherever a complex of the "personal unconscious" has led to an achievement and not to a neurosis, the personality has succeeded spontaneously or reactively in going beyond the "merely personal and familiar" element in the complex to attain a collective significance, i.e., to become creative. But actually, when this happens, the personal complex, e.g., the feeling of inferiority or the mother complex, was only the initial spark that led to the achievement, whether in religion, art, science, politics, or in some other field.

The term "overcompensation" here simply means that the personal complex of the individual, which is a matter of complete indifference to humanity, did not lead to an illness that would also be completely indifferent to mankind, but to something—an accomplishment—that does to a greater or lesser extent concern humanity. The initial spark, e.g., the feeling of inferiority and the related will to power, has not stopped at pathological fantasies; rather, the complex, the wound, has "opened up" some part of the personality to something with an authentic significance for the collectivity. In this connection it is of secondary importance whether something is a content of the collective unconscious or a revaluation of the cultural canon. As we know, every man, sick, normal, or creative, has "complexes," [4] and the question arises: What is it in the reaction of the individual to the complexes of the personal unconscious, which occur in every individual development, that distinguishes the one from the other?

Depth psychology has found that the psychic life of the individual comprises a tendency toward balance and

4. C. G. Jung, "A Review of the Complex Theory."

wholeness of the personality, not only in the second half of life, but from the very start. This tendency toward wholeness compensates for disturbances of development; it supplies largely unconscious countermovements that tend to correct excessive one-sidedness. The law of individual self-regulation, which applies to psychic as well as organic life, is reflected in an attempt to draw the "labile psychic position" indicated by the personal complex into the totality. First of all, fantasies develop around the complex. These fantasies consist in a connection established by the unconscious itself between merely personal complexes and unconscious representations, which are often interpreted as wish images and representations of omnipotence. But too often this interpretation leads one to forget the constructive effect of the fantasies that are always bound up with archetypal contents. These fantasies give the blocked personality a new direction, start the psychic life on a new advance, and cause the individual to become productive. A relation to the primordial image, the archetypal reality, brings about a transformation that must be designated as productive.

In the case of the average, normal development fantasies of salvation or greatness lead, perhaps through a relation with the archetypal hero myth and identification of the ego with the hero, who always archetypally symbolizes consciousness, to the strengthening of the ego that is necessary if the personal complex is to be overcome. In addition these fantasies, under the control of reality, help to foster a natural ambition that leads to cultural achievement. But the control of reality means the acceptance of the cultural canon and its values, to which the ambition now extends. The content of this ambition may vary greatly; it may embody a desire to be "masculine" or "feminine," shrewd, competent, brave, etc.; in other words, it always relates to that part of the cultural canon which is directly connected with the personal complex. This "transformation" might be characterized by the vague term "sublimation," which would here mean a culturization and socialization of the individual, made possible by the connection established between the complexes and the archetypes. In the neurotic who is confined regressively within his fantasy world, this transformation process of the personal complexes is not successful, or only incompletely so; [5] but in the creative man the process takes a different course, as we shall presently see in detail.

The separation between the psychic systems, which becomes intensified in the course of development, leads more and more to a defensive attitude of consciousness over against the unconscious, and to the formation of a cultural canon that is oriented more toward stability of consciousness than toward the transformative phenomena of possession. Ritual, which may be regarded as a central area of psychic transformation, loses its regenerative significance. With the dissolution of the primitive group and the progress of an individualization dominated by ego consciousness, religious ritual and art become ineffectual; and we approach the crisis of modern

5. The reasons for this failure, which are to be sought, for the most part, in disturbances of ego development, cannot concern us here.

man, with his sharp separation of systems, his split between consciousness and unconscious, his neurosis, and his incapacity for total creative transformation.

At this critical point, as we know, a compensatory trend sets in: the individuation process with its individual mythology and individual rites. The problem of individual transformation arises. But here we shall not be concerned with the transformative process that takes place in individuation, with its relation to the universal creative principle and its deviations from it. These matters have been treated exhaustively by Jung.

The modern turn toward creative transformation is manifested not only in analytical psychology but also in the efforts of educators to develop the creative faculty both of children and adults. Domination by our one-sided culture of consciousness has led the individual almost to a sclerosis of consciousness; he has become well-nigh incapable of psychic transformation. In this situation the ego becomes an exclusive ego, a development reflected in such terms as "egoistic" and "egocentric." It becomes closed both to the *thou* of the self, of the individual's own wholeness, and to the *thou* of the outside, of the world and mankind.

This "egoization" of a closed-off and sclerotic consciousness is completed by the formation of an ego ideal. In contradistinction to the self, the center of the real and living totality (i.e., the totality that is transformed and brings transformation), the ego ideal is a function and an artificial product of reaction. It arises in part through the pressure of the collective conscience, the tradition-bound superego, which impresses the values desired by the collective upon the individual and helps to suppress individual traits deviating from the cultural canon. The ego ideal comprises the culture-conditioned will to be different from what one really is, i.e., a conscious and unconscious rejection and repression of the self, which leads both to the sham personality, or persona, and to the splitting-off of the shadow.

The formation of an ego ideal through adaptation to the cultural canon and of the authorities thus necessitated is in itself normal if—and this is the crux of the matter—the experience of the individual self and the bond with the creative, transformative powers of the unconscious remain alive. In the sclerotic consciousness typical of our cultural situation, we have a radicalization of the ego and the ego ideal; egoistic separation from the living unconscious and loss of self have become an acute danger.

Repression by the sclerotic consciousness creates an underworld with a dangerous emotional charge, which tends to erupt, to overpower and destroy the world of the victors; this underworld is inhabited by the vanquished and suppressed gods, the demons and Titans, the dragons, which form the perilous substructure of the dominant world of the victors. But as the myth implies, this repression does not transform the powers; it merely chains them temporarily. The day of judgment, or some other day in the future, brings a twilight of the gods. The victorious gods of consciousness are overthrown, and old Satan, old Loki, the old Titans, break through, unchanged, and as mighty as on the day of their subjection. Seen from the standpoint of this final aspect, when only the intervention of the creative godhead can bring a victory and a new beginning, the entire course of history is meaningless. The antagonisms between the powers that had led to battle and repression remain as intense as they were in the beginning, and the powers that had been repressed but not transformed must again —at least according to an absurd dogma, here simplified—be repressed, but now forever. But only if the saving figure of the redeemer returns, not as a judge, in accordance with the old myth, but, as the new myth seems to say, as one who transforms, can there be a realization of the synthesis toward which the original tension of opposites aimed.

But until then—that is, as long as our reality is dominated not only by a separation of opposites within reality but also by the dangerous splitting-off of the conscious world from the unconscious—evil will appear predominantly, though not exclusively, in two very different but closely related forms. For Satan as antithesis to the primordial living world of transformation is rigidity—the rigidity which our conscious culture, for example, ordains so sternly in its hostility to transformation—but at the same time he appears as its opposite, as chaos.

The rigid, unequivocal self-certainty—in this connection, one should say "ego-certainty"—which excludes transformation and all creativity, including revelation, is a thing of the Devil. Where it prevails, the situation of man, ego, and consciousness is profoundly misunderstood, and the fundamental phenomenon of existence, the phenomenon of change—growth, transformation, passing away—that surrounds the life of every creature is disregarded. The danger of this diabolical rigidity is inherent in all dogmatism, in all bigotry: both are symbols of occlusion to revelation. To have eyes and not see, to have ears and not hear; these are the typical and unmistakable symptoms of occlusion to the call of creative vitality.

But the other side of the Devil, the exact reverse of his rigidity, is chaos. We know only too well by our own example, as individuals and as a whole, how this "other side" of our rigid consciousness looks. We engender within ourselves this structureless, blurred, impure amorphousness, this mass formlessness and aversion to form, wherever the Devil's rigidity dominates our consciousness and our life. The smooth, undifferentiated fixity of the one is inseparable from the molluscous, undifferentiated chaos of the other.

Rigidity and chaos, these two forms of the negative, are directly opposed to the creative principle, which encompasses transformation, hence not only life but also death. Across the diabolical axis of rigidity and chaos cuts the transformative axis of life and death. In the unconscious life of nature these two axes seem to coincide, and what in the extreme case is rigidity appears subsequently as firmness rooted in life. Similarly, what in the extreme is chaos appears normally linked with the principle of death. It is only in man, with his development of consciousness and separation of the systems, that the axes move apart. Chaos and a seemingly unshakable order of consciousness appear only in humankind, for extrahuman nature is as free from the Devil as it is from rigidity and chaos.

For this reason only the experience of our own confused psyche has led us to begin our mythology with a chaos out of which, as we assert in defiance of all probability, order developed. This again is only a projection of our incomplete experience of the genesis of our own order-giving consciousness. Even today our consciousness, in its striving to comprehend itself, has for the most part failed to see that the development of this order and light of consciousness is contingent on a pre-established order and a primordial light.

The order that we find in the unconscious as well as in consciousness—the spiritual order of the instincts, for example—long before the rise of consciousness as a determinant of organic life and its development, lies in a plane of experience to which the normal experience of our polarizing consciousness does not attain. On this plane the human community lives with the relative solidity and security of a world supported by the cultural canon, and only seldom does an earthquake, a subterranean encounter with the repressed powers of chaos, the Titans and the Midgard Serpent, disturb the security of the human collectivity.

The stratum of chaos and the world of a prechaotic order that lives deep down below it are separated from the upper world by a fiery zone of emotions, into which the average individual rightly avoids plunging. In the late period of culture, at least, as long as the points of approach to the powers are solemnized in the cultural canon itself, it suffices for the average man to approach the numinous volcano of the subterranean fire with veneration and at a safe distance. But if, as in our day, the collective road to these regions is no longer viable, we experience their presence primarily in the zones of irruption, to which belong the psychic disorders. Related to these, but essentially different, is the creative process— a fundamental human phenomenon.

We know that phenomena of possession appear also in the creative man. But in the evaluation of the connection between the creative personality and transformation, the individual who stops in his possession and whose productivity is based on a monomania, an *idée fixe,* occupies only a low rank in the hierarchy of creative men, though his achievement may still be significant for the collectivity.

Creative transformation, on the other hand, represents a total process in which the creative principle is manifested, not as an irruptive possession, but as a power related to the self, the center of the whole personality. For partial possession by a single content can be overcome only where the centroversion that makes for wholeness of the personality remains the guiding factor. In this event the law of psychic compensation leads to an unremitting dialectical exchange between the assimilating consciousness and the contents that are continuously being newly constellated. Then begins the continuous process characteristic of creative transformation —new constellations of the unconscious and of consciousness interact with new productions and new transformative phases of the personality. The creative principle thus seizes upon and transforms consciousness as well as the unconscious, the ego-self relation as well as the ego-*thou* relation. For in a creative transformation of the total personality, a modified relation to the *thou* and the world indicates a new relation to the unconscious and the self, and the clearest, though not the only, indication of psychic transformation is a change in the relation to extrapsychic reality.

But objectively the transformative process typical of the creative man is not reflected only in what we call "personal influence." Often enough this personal influence, as the phenomenon of dictators has shown, is based on possession and projections, in other words, on factors of highly dubious origin. In its highest form it belongs to the effects of the creative process; but the phenomenon of the "opus," synthesized from the inside and outside, the psychically subjective and objective, is a more evident part of it. In every field of human culture, the opus is its creator's "child"; it is the product of his individual psychic transformation and wholeness, and at the same time a new objective entity which opens up something to mankind, that is, represents a form of creative revelation.

Precisely because for us the symbol-creating collective forces of myth and religion, rites and festivals, have lost most of their efficacy as cultural phenomena binding upon the collectivity, the creative principle in art has achieved a unique prominence in our time. Art, which up to the Renaissance was almost exclusively the handmaiden of religion, of culture, or of the state, has acquired an ever increasing influence on the consciousness of our day, as the abundance of publications on the art and artists of all times indicates. The extent of the change becomes clear when we consider the social position of so great a genius as Mozart as late as the eighteenth century, and the national or international esteem in which the leading musicians, painters, and writers are held today. The creative individual seems to enjoy such prestige partly because he exemplifies the utmost transformation possible in our time, but above all because the world he creates is an adequate image of the primordial *one* reality, not yet split by consciousness—a reality that only a personality creating from out of its wholeness is able to create.

Differentiation and hyperdifferentiation of consciousness down to the most dangerous one-sidedness and disequilibrium are the hallmarks of our culture, whose faulty balance can no longer be repaired solely by the natural compensation of the psyche. But a return to the old symbols, an attempt to cling to what still remains of the symbolic-religious values, also seems doomed to failure. For our understanding of this symbolism, even our affirmation of it, implies that the symbol itself has departed from the numinous realm of the creative and entered into the sphere of conscious assimilation. And this cannot be altered by our knowledge, born of experience, that the symbol embodies a numinous factor transcending our consciousness. As long as authentic symbolic action is present, an interpretation and a conflict of interpretations are indeed possible—as the history of all religious dogmas bears witness—but the object of controversy is realities and not symbols. To simplify, the disagreements involve the attributes of the godhead, not the symbolism of the representations of God.

The creative principle has its home no longer in the symbolism of a cultural canon, but in the individual. It has almost ceased to live in favored holy places, in sites or at times dedicated to it, or in men consecrated to it, but may live everywhere, anywhere, in any way and any time, that is to say, anonymously. Because in our time the creative principle always hides in an anonymity that discloses its origin by no divine sign, no visible radiance, no demonstrable legitimacy, we have entered upon the spiritual poverty suggested in the Jewish legend about the Messiah in the guise of a beggar, sitting and waiting by the gates of Rome. What is he waiting for? He is waiting for you. This means that creative redemption—and for the Jew, as we know, redemption has not yet come—is disguised as an Everyman, and, what is far more, his poverty and helplessness make him dependent on the devotion that every man accords to this Everyman. This is our situation. We stand before the creative principle. Wherever we find the creative principle, in the Great Individual and in the child, in the sick man or in the simple everyday life, we venerate it as the hidden treasure that in humble form conceals a fragment of the godhead.

If the Old Testament conception of a man made in God's image can be experienced as living reality, it is primarily because man, in addition to being a creature, is also a creative force demanding fulfillment. Wherever it appears, this creative force has a character of revelation, but the revelation is intimately bound up with the psychic structure to which and in which it is revealed. For us the character of revelation is no longer separable from the individual. The creative principle is so deeply rooted in the deepest and darkest corner of his unconscious, and in what is best and highest in his consciousness, that we can comprehend it only as the fruit of his whole existence.

One of the basic fallacies in regard to the creative principle springs from the accent on a human development *progressing* from the unconscious to consciousness. As long as the development of human consciousness is regarded as identical with the differentiation and development of thought, the creative man, as well as the group which in ritual and festival comes into contact with the depths of the unconscious, must appear to be immersing themselves in worlds of archaic primitive symbolism. Even if the regenerative character of this phenomenon is understood—an insight that is often cloaked beneath the notion of sublimation—it is still held that this archaic, regressive mode should and can be overcome with advancing development. This attitude underlies every so-called scientific view of the world, including psychoanalysis, for which all symbolic, creative reality is essentially a "prescientific" phase that must be superseded. For this orientation the highest human type is the exponent of the radically rational consciousness, while the symbol-creating man, though not neurotic, "actually" represents an atavistic human type. In such an approach the nature of the artist, the creator of symbols, is totally misunderstood; his development and creative achievement are derived from a fixation in a childhood phase of development. The symbol, too, is misunderstood and poetry, for example, is reduced to the "magical infantilism" that holds with the "omnipotence of thoughts."

It cannot be stressed enough that the key to a fundamental understanding, not only of man, but of the world as well, is to be sought in the relation between creativity and symbolic reality. Only if we recognize that symbols reflect a more complete reality than can be encompassed in the rational concepts of consciousness can we appreciate the full value of man's power to create symbols. To regard symbolism as an early stage in the development of the rational, conceptual consciousness involves a dangerous underestimation of the makers of symbols and of their functions, without which the human species would be neither capable nor worthy of living.

We do not mean to deny that at certain points the reductive analysis of the creative and noncreative man discloses authentic facts. These personal factors are significant both for the therapy of the sick man and for the biography of the creative man. But analysis of the creative process begins precisely where reductive analysis stops, with the investigation of the connections between personal factors and archetypal contents, that is to say, the contents of the collective unconscious. It is only by virtue of these connections that the individual can become creative and that his work can become significant for the collectivity. Hence a reductive analysis of the creative process and of the creative man is not only false but represents a danger to culture, because it prevents the creative powers from compensating for the culture of consciousness, exacerbates the one-sided development of individual consciousness, and drives both individual and culture to a neurotic cleavage.

And the result of such a development is that even from the standpoint of the one-sided rationalist the reverse of what he had intended happens. For if devaluation of the symbol-creating unconscious brings with it a severe split between the rational consciousness and the unconscious, the ego consciousness, unbeknownst to itself, will be overcome by the powers which it negates and seeks to exclude. Consciousness becomes fanatical and dogmatic; or, in psychological terms, it is overpowered by unconscious contents and unconsciously remythicized. It still recognizes only rational dominants, but in reality it is subjected to processes which, because they are archetypal, are stronger than itself, but which the prejudiced consciousness cannot understand. Consciousness then forms the unconscious religions and myths that we see on a small scale in psychoanalysis and on a large scale in movements such as Nazism and Communism. It is the pseudo-religious background of such dogmatic positions that explains why they are virtually ineradicable. Such dogmas are rooted in archetypal images which consciousness had resolved to exclude; but they are pseudo-religious because, in contrast to authentic religious contents, they lead to a regression and a dissolution of consciousness.

Even if consciousness were justified in regarding the archetypal powers of the unconscious as archaic and hostile to consciousness—though this is by no means the case—it could ensure its development only by "keeping them carefully in mind," for the moment it loses sight of them or regards them as nonexistent, it unconsciously falls a victim to them. When we consider the totality of the human psyche, in which consciousness and the unconscious are interdependent both in their development and in their functions, we see that consciousness can develop only where it preserves a living bond with the creative powers of the unconscious.

The growth of consciousness is not limited to awareness of an "outside world"; in equal measure it comprises an increasing awareness of man's dependence on intrapsychic forces. But this must not be taken as "growing" awareness of a subjective limitation, of a "personal equation" which obscures an objective manifestation of the outside world that we designate as "reality." It must not be forgotten that the outside world that we apprehend with our differentiated consciousness is only a segment of reality, and that our consciousness has developed and differentiated itself as a specialized organ for apprehending this particular segment of reality.

We have elsewhere shown in detail [6] that we pay a heavy price for the sharpness of our conscious knowledge, which is based on the separation of the psychic systems and which breaks down the one world into the polarity of psyche and world. This price is a drastic curtailment of the reality that we experience. And we also pointed out that the experience of this one reality is a qualitatively different form of experience, which seems

6. See my "Die Psyche und die Wandlung der Wirklichkeitsebenen."

"indistinct" from the standpoint of the developed consciousness.

The experience of the one reality, which both phylogenetically and ontogenetically precedes the experience of reality by the differentiated consciousness, is eminently "symbolic." Early psychologists looked back from the vantage point of the differentiated consciousness and dissected the symbol into its components, in the belief that something inward was projected outward. More recently we have come to view symbolic experience as a primary existence: the one reality is experienced adequately and as a whole by a psyche that has not yet been split by the separation of the systems, or that has ceased to be split. Formerly it was thought, for example, that the symbolic perception of a tree involved an outward projection of an interior something; one projected a psychic image upon the tree, the object outside. But this thesis has proved untenable, although it seemed plausible to the ego consciousness of modern man, who experiences the one world as split into an inside and an outside.

Actually, for ourselves as well as for primitive man, there is not a tree object outside and a tree image inside, which may be regarded as photographs of one another. The personality as a whole is oriented toward the one reality, and its primary experience of the intrinsically unknown part of that reality that we call a tree is symbolic. In other words, the feeling-toned experience of the symbol with its sense content is something primary and synthetic; it is a unitary image of one part of the unitary world. Inward and outward "perceptual images," on the other hand, are secondary and derived. An indication of this is that the science of our isolated and isolating consciousness still discovers vestiges of symbols in our perceptual images and strives to move us into an imageless world that can only be thought. But even then our psyche persists in perceiving images, and we continue to experience symbols, though now they are scientific and mathematical symbols. But the greatest of our scientists and mathematicians experience these symbolic abstractions of consciousness as something numinous; the emotional factor in the subject, previously excluded from scientific inquiry as a matter of principle, reappears, "so to speak, in the object."

The development of the intrinsically unknown substance, of the intrinsically unknown and unrepresentable one world, brings with it a confrontation and a differentiation; with the help of images the psyche so orients itself in, and adapts itself to, the world as to become capable of life and development. For this reason we call these images "adequate to the world." This development comprises symbolic images in which parts of the one reality are perceived. The subsequent process of conscious differentiation, with its dual schema of inside and outside, psyche and world, splits the unitary symbolic image in two: on the one hand an inward, "psychic" image, on the other an outward, "physical" image. Actually neither can be derived from the other, for both are partial images of an original symbolic unity that has been split in two. The tree outside is just as much an image as is the tree inside. To the tree outside "corresponds" an unrepresentable part of the unitary reality, which can be experienced only with relative adequacy in the image; while to the tree inside corresponds a part of the experiencing, living substance, which again is experienced only with relative adequacy. We cannot derive the inward partial tree image from the tree outside, for we experience the latter too as an image; nor can we derive the outward partial tree image from the projection of an inward image, since this inward partial image is just as primary as the outward one. Both spring from the primary symbolic image—tree—which is more adequate to the unitary reality than are its partial derivatives, the inward and outward image relating to the secondary, divided world.

But the "primary symbolic image" is not complex, or alien to our experience. In a certain state of mind, which may be brought on in a number of ways, the "object vis-à-vis" becomes transformed for us. The term *participation mystique* has a very similar implication, but was coined for something remote from the experience of modern man. When things, a landscape or a work of art, come alive or "grow transparent," [7] this signifies that they are transformed into what we have called "unitary reality." What we see becomes "symbolic" in the sense that it speaks to us in a new way, that it reveals something unknown, and that in its actual presence, just as it is, it is at the same time something entirely different: the categories of "being" and "meaning" coincide.

A passage in Huxley's *The Doors of Perception* will make my meaning clear. A psychic transformation, artificially induced by the drug mescaline, has led the author to a symbolic perception of the one reality.

7. See "Art and Time" in this volume, p. 105.

"I was not looking now at an unusual flower arrangement. I was seeing what Adam had seen on the morning of his creation—the miracle, moment by moment, of naked existence.

" 'Is it agreeable?' somebody asked. (During this part of the experiment, all conversations were recorded on a dictating machine, and it has been possible for me to refresh my memory of what was said.)

" 'Neither agreeable nor disagreeable,' I answered. 'It just *is*.'

"*Istigkeit*—wasn't that the word Meister Eckhart liked to use? 'Is-ness.' The Being of Platonic philosophy— except that Plato seems to have made the enormous, the grotesque mistake of separating Being from becoming and identifying it with the mathematical abstraction of the Idea. He could never, poor fellow, have seen a bunch of flowers shining with their own inner light and all but quivering under the pressure of the significance with which they were charged; could never have perceived that what rose and iris and carnation so intensely signi-fied was nothing more, and nothing less, than what they were—a transience that was yet eternal life, a perpetual perishing that was at the same time pure Being, a bundle of minute, unique particulars in which, by some un-speakable and yet self-evident paradox, was to be seen the divine source of all existence." [8]

This insight into the symbolic mode that preceded our consciousness seems to justify our theoretical digres-sion. For it turns out that the vision and production of a symbolic world of the archetypal as well as natural in

8. Aldous Huxley, *The Doors of Perception*, p. 17.

religion, rite, myth, art, and festival not only involve an atavistic factor and a regenerative element arising from their emotional charge. In a certain sense they are characterized precisely by the fact that in them a fragment of the unitary reality is apprehended—a deeper, more primordial, and at the same time more complete reality that we are fundamentally unable to grasp with our differentiated conscious functions, because their development is oriented toward a sharper perception of sections of polarized reality. In the differentiation of consciousness we seem to be doing the same thing as when we close our eyes in order to enhance our hearing, in order that we may be "all ears." Unquestionably this exclusion sharpens and intensifies our hearing. But in thus excluding the other senses we perceive only a segment of the total sensory reality, which we experience more adequately and fully if we not only hear it but also see, smell, taste, and touch it.

There is nothing mystical about the symbolical unitary reality, and it is not beyond our experience; it is the world that is always experienced where the polarization of inside and outside, resulting from the separation of the psychic systems, has not yet been effected or is no longer in force. It is the authentic, total world of transformation as experienced by the creative man.

II

Every transformative or creative process comprises stages of possession. To be moved, captivated, spellbound, signify to be possessed by something; and without such a fascination and the emotional tension connected with it, no concentration, no lasting interest, no creative process, are possible. Every possession can justifiably be interpreted either as a one-sided narrowing or as an intensification and deepening. The exclusivity and radicality of such "possession" represent both an opportunity and a danger. But no great achievement is possible if one does not accept this risk, though the notion of "acceptance of the risk" implied in the hero myth presupposes far more freedom than the overpowered ego actually possesses. The workings of the autonomous complexes presuppose a disunity of the psyche, whose integration is an endless process. The world and the collective unconscious in which the individual lives are fundamentally beyond his mastery; the most he can do is to experience and integrate more and more parts of them. But the unintegrated factors are not only a cause for alarm; they are also the source of transformation.

It is not only the "great" contents of world and psyche, the fateful irruptions and archetypal experiences, that bear within them the seeds of transformation; the "complexes," the partial souls that are not merely hostile disorders but natural components of our psyche, are also positive movers and begetters of transformation.

We have pointed out that normally the individual adapts himself to the cultural canon by way of the link between the complexes and the archetypes. As consciousness develops, the childlike psyche's bond with the archetypes is continuously replaced by personal relations with the environment, and the tie with the great archetypes of childhood is transferred to the archetypal canon of the prevailing culture. This occurs through increasing emphasis on the ego, on consciousness and the environment. The world of childhood, with its stress on totality, on direct contact with the self, is repressed in favor of normal adaptation. In the creative man, too, a link arises between personal complexes and archetypal images. But in him it is not assimilated, as in the normal man, through adaptation to the principle of reality as represented by the cultural canon.

As we know, psychoanalysis attempts to derive creativity from a constitutional deficiency. By way of simplification this might be called an excess of libido, which causes a personally unfulfilled childhood and a fixation in it. All the schemata valid for the average man—pre-Oedipal fixation, castration anxiety, superego formation, and Oedipus complex—are applied unchanged to the creative man; but his excess of libido and its supposed "sublimation" are made responsible for the abnormal solution of his childhood problem and for his achievement. In this view the creative man represents a highly dubious variant of human nature; he remains fixated in childhood, and never grows beyond the prescientific stage of symbolism. Sublimation and recognition by the collectivity would then signify that the artist helps all men to enjoy a pretty-well-concealed infantilism—and this is called secondary elaboration. In art men abreact their own infantile complexes, looking on as Oedipus, Hamlet, or Don Carlos slays his own father. (But even in the normal man these schemata, here construed personalistically, are related to archetypal constellations that reach much deeper.)

Yet the difference between the creative and the normal man does not, as the psychoanalytical school supposes, consist in a surplus of libido; it resides in an intensified psychic tension that is present in the creative man from the very start. In him a special animation of the unconscious and an equally strong emphasis on the ego and its development are demonstrable at an early stage.

This acute psychic tension and an ego that suffers from it reflect the creative man's special kind of alertness. He usually possesses it even as a child, but this alertness is not identical with the reflecting consciousness of a precocious intellect. The childhood state of the creative individual can be characterized no better than in Hölderlin's words: "und schlummert wachenden Schlaf" ("and slumbers in waking sleep").[9] In this state of alertness the child is open to a world, to an overwhelming unitary reality that surpasses and overpowers him on all sides. At once sheltered and exposed, this waking sleep, for which there is as yet no outside and no inside, is the unforgettable possession of the creative man. It is the period in which the whole and undivided world, infinite and beyond the compass of the ego, stands behind every pain and every joy. In this childlike experience every personal content is bound up with a transpersonal archetypal content, while, on the other hand, the transpersonal and archetypal are always situated in the personal. Once we appreciate what it means to experience such a unity of the transpersonal and personal, in which ego and man-

9. "At the Source of the Danube," in *Hölderlin* (tr. Michael Hamburger), p. 169.

kind are still one, we begin to wonder how it is possible, by what paths and what exertions, to overcome and forget this fundamental experience, as the average man succeeds in doing with the help of his education; and we cease to marvel that the creative man should remain fixated in this stage and its experiences.

From childhood onward the creative individual is captivated by his experience of the unitary reality of childhood; he returns over and over again to the great hieroglyphic images of archetypal existence. They were mirrored for the first time in the well of childhood and there they remain until, recollecting, we bend over the rim of the well and rediscover them, forever unchanged.

It is true that all the normal tendencies are likewise present in the creative man and that he realizes them to a certain extent, but this individual destiny cuts across his normal development. Because his nature prevents him from accomplishing the normal development of the average man, with its prescribed adaptation to reality, even his youth is often abnormal both in a good and a bad sense. His conflict with his environment often begins at an early age with an intensity that seems pathological, for precisely in childhood and youth the creative and the abnormal or pathological are close together. For, in opposition to the demands of the cultural canon, the creative man holds fast to the archetypal world and to his original bisexuality and wholeness, or, in other words, to his self.

This constellation of the creative man appears at first as a fixation in the childhood milieu and the fateful persons and places of childhood. But here, even more

than in other childhoods, the personal is always inter-
mingled with the suprapersonal, the personal locality
with an invisible world. And this world is not merely a
"childlike" world; it is the true, the real, or, as Rilke
called it, the "open" world.

> Love, the possessive, encircles
> the child for ever betrayed in secret;
> and pledges it to a future that's not its own.

> Afternoons when, left to itself, it kept looking from mirror
>     to mirror,
> staring; when it kept asking itself the riddle
> of its own name: Who? Who?—But the others
> return home and overwhelm it.
> What the window, what the path,
> what the stuffy smell of a drawer confided
> to it yesterday: they drown with their presence, frustrate.
> Once more it is their possession.
> Sprays will at times fling themselves out from the denser
> bushes in the way its desire flings out
> from the tangle of family, swaying into clearness.
> But day by day they keep blunting its glance on their wonted
> walls, that upward glance which encounters dogs
> and has taller flowers
> nearly opposite time and again.[10]

But openness—here we speak of the boy, whose creativity is easier to understand than that of the girl—always coincides with femininity. In the creative man this
feminine principle, this motive of transformation, which
in the normal adult becomes discernible as an "anima,"

10. R. M. Rilke, *Correspondence in Verse with Erika Mitterer*
(tr. N. K. Cruickshank), p. 35.

is usually associated with the image of the maternal.[11] It makes the child receptive, open to suffering and experience, but also to what is great and overpowering in the world; it keeps alive the stream that pours in on him from without. It is only too easy to understand that this constellation must be rich in conflicts and must make adaptation difficult unless nature has been particularly kind in its mixing of the elements.

In every creative individual the accent is unquestionably on the receptive component from the very start, but we must not forget that this same accent prevails in the child, and that a great struggle is often required before it can be overcome by an education oriented toward the sexually one-sided cultural values. But on the other hand, the preservation of a certain receptivity is at the same time a preservation of one's own individuality, an alertness toward one's own self—whether experienced as hardship, as mission, or as necessity—which now comes into conflict with the world, with convention, with the cultural canon, or, according to the ancient pattern of the hero myth, with the traditional father image. And because the dominance of the primary archetypal world is preserved and not replaced by that of the cultural canon, the development of personality and consciousness is subject to a different law than in the normal man.

The dominance of the mother archetype in numerous writers and artists is not adequately explained by the child's relation to his personal mother. We find good as well as bad relationships; we find mothers who have

11. See "Leonardo da Vinci and the Mother Archetype" in this volume.

died young and mothers who have lived to a ripe old age; we find mothers with imposing as well as insignificant personalities. The reason for this—as the psychoanalysts recognized—is that the determining factor is the child's and not the adult ego's relation to the mother. But the small child's relation to his mother is molded by the mother archetype, which is always blended with the mother imago, the subjective image of the experience of the personal mother.

In the course of normal development the importance of the mother archetype diminishes; a personal relation to the personal mother takes form, and through it the individual develops a large part of his capacity for relations with the world and with his fellow men in general. Where this relation is impaired, the consequences are neuroses and fixation in the phase of the original mother relation, when something requisite to the healthy development of the individual was not accomplished. But when the archetypal mother image remains dominant and the individual does not fall sick, we have one of the fundamental constellations of the creative process.

We have elsewhere pointed out the significance of the mother archetype for the creative man; here I wish only to stress that the Good (or the Terrible) Mother is among other things a symbol for the determining influence of the archetypal world as a whole, an influence that may reach down to the biopsychical level. The prevalence of the Great Mother archetype marks the prevalence of the archetypal world, which is the foundation of all development of consciousness, of the childhood world, in which the phylogenetic development of consciousness and the ego is repeated ontogenetically from out of the primordial archetypal world.

The transition from the personal complex by way of the predominantly archetypal fantasy world to consciousness leads normally to a recession of the individual's tendency to wholeness in favor of an ego development that is guided by the cultural canon and the collective consciousness—by the superego of ancestral tradition and the introjected conscience. The creative man, however, is stigmatized by his failure to abandon the self's directive toward wholeness in order to adapt himself to the reality of the environment and its dominant values. The creative man, like the hero of myth, stands in conflict with the world of the fathers, i.e., the dominant values, because in him the archetypal world and the self that directs it are such overpowering, living, direct experiences that they cannot be repressed. The normal individual is released from his heroic mission by his institutional education toward identification with the father archetype, and so becomes a well-adjusted member of his patriarchally directed group. In the creative man, however, with his predominant mother archetype, the uncertain, wavering ego must itself take the exemplary, archetypal way of the hero; must slay the father, dethrone the conventional world of the traditional canon, and seek an unknown directing authority, namely, the self that is so hard to experience, the unknown Heavenly Father.

In the creative individual, regardless of biographical details, reductive analysis will almost invariably discover mother fixation and parricide, i.e., Oedipus complex;

185

"family romance," i.e., the search for the unknown father; and narcissism, i.e., preservation of a relation to himself in opposition to love of the environment and of an outside object.

This relation of the creative man to himself involves an enduring and insuperable paradox. This type's innate receptivity makes him suffer keenly from his personal complexes. But from the very outset this suffering, because he always experiences his personal complexes along with their archetypal correspondences, is not only a private and personal suffering but at the same time a largely unconscious existential suffering from the fundamental human problems that constellate themselves in every archetype.

Consequently, the individual history of every creative man is always close to the abyss of sickness; he does not, like other men, tend to heal the personal wounds involved in all development by an increased adaptation to the collectivity. His wounds remain open, but his suffering from them is situated in depths from which another curative power arises, and this curative power is the creative process.

As the myth puts it, only a wounded man can be a healer, a physician.[12] Because in his own suffering the creative man experiences the profound wounds of his collectivity and his time, he carries deep within him a regenerative force capable of bringing forth a cure not only for himself but also for the community.

This complex sensibility of the creative man increases his dependence on the center of wholeness, the self,

12. C. Kerényi, *Asklepios: Archetype of the Physician's Existence.*

which, in continuous attempts at compensation, enhances the ego development and ego stability that must provide a counterweight to the archetypal preponderance. In the perpetual tension between an animated and menacing archetypal world and an ego reinforced for purposes of compensation, but possessing no support in the conventional father archetype, the ego can lean only upon the self, the center of individual wholeness, which, however, is always infinitely more than individual.

One of the paradoxes of the creative man's existence is that he experiences his attachment to his ego almost as a sin against the suprapersonal power of the archetypes that hold him in their grip. Nevertheless, he knows that this is the only possible means of enabling himself and the powers that command him to take form and express themselves. This fundamental fact constellates the profound personal ambivalence of the creative man, but through it he achieves individuation in his work, since he is always compelled to seek the center if he is to exist. Whereas a normal life, in accordance with the dictates of the ego ideal, demands repression of the shadow, the life of the creative man is shaped both by the suffering that knows itself and by the pleasure-toned creative expression of the totality, the pleasure-giving ability to let what is lowest and highest in him live and take form together.

This phenomenon of formation from out of the whole has nothing to do with "sublimation" in the usual sense, and it is also meaningless to reduce this totality to infantile components; for example, to derive the fundamental fact that the creative man expresses something of himself, that an essential part of his individual subjectivity is manifested in his work, from exhibitionism. Such a reduction is no more justified than the churlish and absurd attempt to explain Rilke's habit, of "carrying his material around with him for years before giving it final form and parting with it," on the basis of anal eroticism.[13]

For in the creative man attitudes that in the infant and child appear on the physical plane as universally human phenomena, and in the sick man are likewise fixated in this plane as perversions and symptoms, cease to express themselves or at least to find their chief expression on this plane. They have achieved a totally different and new level of psychic expression and meaning; they not only mean but also *are* something different.

Nearly forty years ago Jung established that the predisposition of the child was not polymorphously perverse but rather polyvalent, and that, as he then put it, "even in adult life the vestiges of infantile sexuality are the seeds of vital spiritual functions." [14] Today, for reasons that it would take us too far afield to explain, I prefer to speak not of infantile sexuality, but rather of infantile experiences on the bodily plane. Such experiences always contain both archetypal and worldly factors. For the child, as for early man, there is no such thing as a "merely" bodily factor; his experience of the unitary world regularly includes what we later describe as symbolically significant elements.

13. E. Simenauer, *Rainer Maria Rilke, Legende und Mythos,* p. 596.
14. Jung, "Psychic Conflicts in a Child," Foreword.

The normal individual has the same experience, in sexuality, for example, where the personal and the archetypal, the bodily, psychic, and spiritual, are, momentarily at least, experienced as a unity. This enhanced experience of unity is analogous to that of the child and the creative man. The creative process is synthetic, precisely in that the transpersonal, i.e., the eternal, and the personal, i.e., the ephemeral, merge, and something utterly unique happens: the enduring and eternally creative is actualized in the ephemeral creation. By comparison everything that is solely personal is perishable and insignificant; everything that is solely eternal is inherently irrelevant because inaccessible to us. For every experience of the transpersonal is a limited revelation, i.e., a manifestation according to the modality and scope of our vessel-like power of comprehension.

For the creative man this is fundamental—regardless of whether or not he is aware of it. He opens himself to the transpersonal; or, one might better say, only that man is creative who holds himself open to the transpersonal, that man from whom the period of childhood experience, which takes this openness to the transpersonal for granted, has not departed. This, it should be added, has nothing to do with an interest in childhood or conscious knowledge of it. What has always been regarded as childlike in the creative man is precisely his openness to the world, an openness for which the world is each day created anew. And it is this that makes him perpetually aware of his obligation to purify and broaden his own quality as a vessel, to give adequate expression to what pours in on him, and to fuse the archetypal and eternal with the individual and ephemeral.

In Leonardo, in Goethe, Novalis, or Rilke, for example, the experience of the child, which normally remains mute, and the archetype of the Great Mother, otherwise known to us only from the history of primitive man and of religion, take on new life. They no longer coincide with the archaic image of early mankind but have also encompassed the entire subsequent development of human consciousness and spirit. The image of the mother archetype to which creative form has been given always discloses archaic, symbolic traits, which it has in common with the mother image of early mankind and early childhood. But Leonardo's nature goddess and St. Anne, Goethe's nature and Eternal Feminine, Novalis' night and Madonna, Rilke's night and feminine loving one, are all creative new forms of the One; they are supreme and ultimate new statements. Behind them stands the "eternal presence" of the archetype, but at the same time the creative man— and therein lies his achievement—experiences and lends form to this "eternity" as something which eternally changes and takes on new form, and through which his time and himself are at the same time transformed.

One of the fundamental facts of creative existence is that it produces something objectively significant for culture, but that at the same time these achievements always represent subjective phases of an individual development, of the individuation of the creative man. The psyche carries on its creative struggle "against the stream" of normal direct adaptation to the collectivity;

but what began as compensation of the personal complex by the archetype leads to a continuous activation and animation of the archetypal world as a whole, which henceforth holds the creative man fast. One archetype leads to another, related one, so that the continuously renewed claims of the archetypal world can be satisfied only through continuous transformation of the personality and creative achievement.

Because the creative individual undertakes, or rather is subjected to, this constant struggle with the archetypal world, he becomes the instrument of the archetypes that are constellated in the unconscious of the pertinent collectivity, and that are absolutely necessary to the collectivity by way of compensation.[15] But despite the significance of the creative man for his time, he is far from always achieving direct and immediate influence, not to mention recognition by his contemporaries. And this discrepancy, which in no way argues against the creative individual's essential function for the community, inevitably compels him to preserve, and indeed to fight for, his autonomy over against the collectivity. Thus the objective as well as the subjective situation we have stressed throws the creative man back on himself. His resulting aloofness from his environment and his fellow men can easily be misinterpreted as narcissism. But here we must learn to distinguish between the maladjustment of the neurotic, whose ego fixation makes him almost incapable of relations with others, and the maladjustment of the creative man, whose self-fixation impedes his relations with his fellow men.

15. Cf. "Art and Time."

The symbolism of the creative process contains something regenerative for its epoch; it is the seedbed of future development. But this is possible only because what emerges in the creative work is not only individual but also archetypal, a part of the unitary reality that is enduring and imperishable, since in it the real, the psychic, and the spiritual are still one.

The creative process effected in the tension between the unconscious and the ego-centered consciousness represents a direct analogy to what Jung described as the transcendent function. The hierarchy of creative processes hinges on the varying degree to which the ego and consciousness are drawn into them. When the unconscious produces something without participation of the ego, or where the ego remains purely passive, we have a low level of creativity; the level rises with increasing tension between ego and unconscious. But the transcendent function and the unifying symbol can appear only where there is a tension between a stable consciousness and a "charged" unconscious. Such a constellation normally leads to repression of the one pole: to victory of the stable consciousness, or to capitulation of consciousness and a victory of the unconscious position. Only if this tension is endured—and this always calls forth a state of suffering—can a third term be born, which "transcends," or surpasses, the opposites and so combines parts of both positions into an unknown, new creation.

"The living symbol cannot come to birth in an inert or poorly developed mind, for such a man will rest content with the already existing symbols offered by established tradition. Only the passionate yearning of a highly developed mind, for whom the dictated symbol no longer contains the highest reconciliation in one expression, can create a new symbol. But, inasmuch as the symbol proceeds from his highest and latest mental achievement and must also include the deepest roots of his being, it cannot be a one-sided product of the most highly differentiated mental functions, but must at least have an equal source in the lowest and most primitive motions of his psyche. For this co-operation of antithetic states to be at all possible, they must both stand side by side in fullest conscious opposition. Such a condition necessarily entails a violent disunion with oneself, even to a point where thesis and antithesis mutually deny each other, while the ego is still forced to recognize its absolute participation in both." [16]

The one pole of this tension is provided by the consciousness of the creative man, by his will and intention to produce a work. Normally he is not without purpose and direction. But independently of his intention, as we know from innumerable statements of creative men, the unconscious often breaks through with a "will of its own," which by no means coincides with the will of the artist. (To mention but one example, Thomas Mann's Joseph cycle, first planned as a short story, was to grow into a long novel and exact ten years of effort.) But despite this autonomy of the unconscious, the archetypal world does not stand here in a hostile polar tension to consciousness; for a part of the creative man's consciousness is always receptive, permeable, and turned toward

16. Jung, *Psychological Types*, def. "Symbol."

193

the unconscious. Thus in the greatest of creative men the contents repressed by the collective consciousness do not emerge as hostile powers, for they too are constellated by the creative man's self, his wholeness.

The creative man's bond with the root and foundation of the collectivity is perhaps most beautifully expressed in Hölderlin's words: "The thoughts of the communal spirit come to a quiet end in the poet's soul." [17] But the creative man's product, as part of his development, is always bound up with his "mere individuality," his childhood, his personal experience, his ego's tendencies toward love and hate, his heights and his shadow. For the alertness of his consciousness permits the creative man more than the average man to "know himself" and "suffer from himself." His lasting dependence on his self fortifies him against seduction by a collective ego ideal, but makes him all the more sensitive to the realization that he is inadequate to himself, to the "self." Through this suffering from his shadow, from the wounds that have been open since childhood—these are the gates through which flows the stream of the unconscious, yet the ego never ceases to suffer from them— the creative man arrives at the humility that prevents him from overestimating his ego, because he knows that he is too much at the mercy of his wholeness, of the unknown self within him.

His childlike nature as well as his inadequacy to the world forever kindle his memory of a primordial world and a happy feeling that he may, from time to time at least, show himself adequate or at least receptive to this

17. "To the Poets" (tr. Hamburger), p. 163.

world. But in the creative man, receptivity and the suffering that comes of a higher sensibility are not limited to childhood and the archetypal, to the "real," the "great," one might almost say the "worthy," world that has been experienced in it. Always and everywhere, to be sure, he is driven to rediscover, to reawaken, to give form to this world. But he does not find this world as though seeking something outside him; rather, he knows that this encounter with full reality, the one world, in which everything is still "whole," is bound up with his own transformation toward wholeness. For this reason he must, in every situation, in every constellation, refresh the openness into which alone the open world can enter.

But although, particularly in the greatest creative men, the process of formation is often long and arduous, requiring the most strenuous effort on the part of the ego and of consciousness, the finding of one's depth and the being-found by it are, like every authentic transformative process, neither an act of the will nor of magic, but an event that takes place by the grace of God. This does not lessen the weight of the opus, but on the contrary enhances it; since in the mysterious correspondence between self and ego, the ego, whether rightly or wrongly, associates its own responsibility for the work with its own guilt and unreadiness.

Although the creative process is often pleasure-toned and is not always dominated by suffering, the inward tension or suffering of the psyche forms the problem that is creatively solved only in production. In this suffering which the creative man must experience in his unremitting struggle with the unconscious and himself, the ascending transformation that constitutes his individuation process assimilates all the flaws, defeats, failures, hardships, misery, and sickness of human life, which are normally thrust aside and given over to the shadow and the Devil as negative elements opposed to the ego ideal.

But the unity of ego and self that determines the creative process as such also contains the zones of rigidity and chaos that threaten the life of the conscious man. In the creative sphere they give rise to a third term, which embraces and transcends them both, and this is form. Both antitheses have a part in it, for rigidity and chaos are the two poles that are joined together in form, and form is menaced from both sides, by sclerosis and by chaotic disintegration.

But it is not only in the bonds of form that the negative is redeemed. For the creative man always finds a source of growth and transformation in his own shadow and deficiency.

> For we to what disturbs us, makes afraid,
> owe from the first such boundless obligation.
> Death always took a part in its creation:
> that's how the so unheard-of song was made.[18]

Here "death" means the terrible and the perilous as well as the barriers of human weakness. It is everything that strikes the ego as suffering and ruin. In praising death as the prerequisite of every transformation that merges life and death, the poet allies himself with the creative

18. Rilke, *Correspondence in Verse with Erika Mitterer* (tr. Cruickshank), p. 85.

God himself, the God of transformation who bestows and *is* life and death.

The creative man experiences both the godhead and himself as changing, as willing transformation in creation. And the poet is speaking both of the godhead and himself when he puts these words in the mouth of the Creator:

> For there is an impulse in my works
> That drives toward an increasing transformation.[19]

At the risk of concluding one incomplete statement with another, I should like to close my remarks with an analysis of one of Rilke's poems. An interpretation of a poem can never offer more than a hint, an intimation; but what may justify our attempt is that this poem has given unique expression to the relationships with which we have been concerned today.

The poem in question is the twelfth sonnet in the second series of the *Sonnets to Orpheus:*

Strive for transformation, O be inspired with the flame
Wherein, rich in changes, a thing withdraws from your
   reach;
the planning spirit who masters everything earthly,
loves above all in the sweep of the figure the point where it
   turns.

What locks itself in endurance grows rigid; sheltered
in unassuming grayness, does it feel safe?
Wait, from the distance hardness is menaced by something
   still harder.
Alas—: a remote hammer is poised to strike.

19. Rilke, "Die Worte des Herrn an Johannes auf Patmos," *Gedichte 1906–1926,* p. 571. (Unpublished tr. by J. M. Cohen.)

Knowledge knows him who pours forth as a spring;
Delighted she guides him, showing him what was created in
    joy
And often concludes with beginning and starts with the end.

Every happy space they traverse in wonder
Is child or grandchild of parting. And Daphne, transformed,
feeling herself laurel, wants you to change into wind.[20]

A critic has written: "One might be tempted to relate this poem to Goethe's words about recreating creation lest it arm itself in rigidity."[21] But the second stanza of the sonnet has nothing to do with Goethe's nature that contains life and death, but is based on the apocalyptic experience of vision; it is not a statement of an anonymous principle but is made in the name of the God who proclaimed to St. John on Patmos:

> To me learning is as nothing,
> for I am the fall of fire
> and my glance is forks, like lightning.
> See, I never let it linger.[22]

And in the lines

>           O be inspired with the flame
> Wherein, rich in changes, a thing withdraws from your
>     reach,

we seem to hear an intimation of Goethe's "blessed yearning," but here again Rilke is concerned with some-

20. Rilke, *Die Sonette an Orpheus,* Zweiter Teil, XII. (Unpublished tr. by Ruth Speirs.)

21. K. Kippenberg's postscript to the *Duineser Elegien—Die Sonette an Orpheus.*

22. "Die Worte des Herrn an Johannes auf Patmos," *Gedichte 1906–1926,* p. 572 (tr. Cohen).

thing else. The deadly flame brings radiant transformation, but it is only in its drawing away from us that the thing can be transformed; only in its "becoming invisible" that the miracle occurs.

We have opposed the life- and death-containing principle of transformation to rigidity and chaos. In this poem these antitheses are raised, as it were, to the realm of the invisible; the flame consumes their substance, as God says to John on Patmos:

> And I taste one of their objects
> to see if I shall accept it—
> If it takes fire, it is real.[23]

Only in self-sacrifice, in death by the searing flame, does the thing prove its authenticity. The "strive for transformation" of the first line (more literally, "will transformation") applies only to him who is wholly prepared in his self-abnegation. For transformation, this thing that happens in opposition to all will, can only be "willed" where there is readiness to die. The man of deep insight knows that authentic life is not lived arbitrarily but is governed by a secret mesh of invisible images: "For we live truly in figures"; [24] but even this seems like almost too much certainty, too much of the "enduring," for "in the sweep of the figure" the godhead loves above all "the point where it turns."

Here flame and sacrifice mean nothing hostile to the world and the earth, but—although we have used the word—neither do they mean a sacrifice in the usual

23. Ibid., p. 572.
24. *Die Sonette an Orpheus,* Erster Teil, XII (tr. Speirs).

199

sense. The meaning is closer to that contained in the Hebrew root of the word *sacrifice:* קרב, namely, "to come near," to approach God. It is in this approach to God that the soul takes fire, but the deadly blaze is precisely the turning point, in which life springs from death. For existence at the point where the figure turns, as the strange and profound metaphor of the poem has it, is also a pouring forth, a spring. The spirit that devises projects loves the point where the figure turns and Knowledge knows him "who pours forth as a spring."

Like the act of generation, the essential, creative act in which the spring pours forth contains a sacrifice and an approach as well as a coincidence of life and death. This midpoint between oppositions, in which the tension is gathered into a third and higher term, is such a "turning point." The never-resting flow of the spring is eternal transformation, and as birth and death it is also enduring life, in which there is nothing that endures. Precisely the involuntary character of the flowing reveals the grace of transformation that, as though coming from afar, enters into man and passes through him. Thus the creative man knows himself to be a "mouth," through which passes what has arisen in his innermost earthen night. In this flowing of creativity occurs the essential, which is not embodied in its origin, for that is a "secret," or in the creation, which is enduring and therefore fated to die. Only the source point, in which the stream emerges from darkness and enters the light, and is both at once, darkness and light, is the turning point of transition and transformation. It cannot be looked for and cannot be held; in every moment it is creation from nothingness, independent of its history, and as pure present it is independent of its past as well as its future.

It is this flow that "Knowledge knows." This knowledge embraces God's knowledge of the known; but in it one also senses some force that animates him who pours forth as a spring. The turning point and the spring that pours forth are a duality encountered by the duality of the loving and knowing God. Yet in this supreme drama of love between godhead and man, in this drama of creativeness, he who turns and is transformed, who pours forth as a spring, is not a counterpart of the godhead; he is a medium through which it passes, its mouth and expression. For what turns and pours forth in him is the godhead itself. And nevertheless this knowledge of the earthly still has the Biblical sense of a begetting—a connection so fundamental that even a zoologist, far enough removed from the text of the Hebrew Bible to be regarded as unprejudiced, writes: "The encounter that leads to procreation presupposes a simple kind of 'knowledge' of what belongs together, a finding of beings of the same variety." [25]

It is the same drama that is enacted between the divine knower and the earthly known, who in his self-sacrificing flow both is and becomes creative. For what happens here is what happened at the beginning of time: the creation of the world. And accordingly:

. . . she guides him, showing him what was created in joy
And often concludes with beginning and starts with the end.

25. Adolf Portmann, *Das Tier als soziales Wesen*, p. 115.

And again, in this primordial act of having become creative, of world creation, such a "turning point" is achieved, in which creator and creature, as well as the acts of being begotten and born and becoming creative, merge with one another. The creative process is generation and birth as well as transformation and rebirth. As the Chinese said: "Transformation is the creation of creating." [26] The rapture of him who pours forth like a spring is reflected in the serenity of the creation. The perpetual self-renewal and dependence on grace of him who pours forth eternally are a human parallel to the eternal rebirth of all that is created. The rapture of the flowing deathlessness of creativity is just as much at work in man as in nature; indeed, it is only in his creative flowing that man becomes a part of nature, is joined once more to the "one reality" of existence, in which no enduring thing can endure, because all is transformation.

"The soul," said Heraclitus, "has its own Law (*Logos*), which increases itself (*i.e., grows according to its needs*)." [27] These words express what Philo and the Church Fathers said about the Logos born from the soul, and what the mystics knew of the generative word and the Holy Ghost of speech; but the archetypal meaning of this creative utterance goes deeper. The Biblical myth of the creation of the world by the word of God, and the "word magic" known to us from primitive psy-

26. Hellmut Wilhelm, *Change: Eight Lectures on the I Ching.*
27. Kathleen Freeman, *Ancilla to the Pre-Socratic Philosophers,* p. 32.

chology, both embody the strange unity in which to speak, to know, and to beget-create are still one. This notion of the creative word springs from one of the profoundest experiences of mankind, the realization that a creative, psychic force, reaching out far beyond the individual man, "speaks" in the poet. The images that burst forth in the man gripped by the depths, the song that is their expression in words, are the creative source of nearly all human culture; [28] and an essential part of all religion, art, and customs sprang originally from this dark phenomenon of creative unity in the human soul. Primitive man regarded this creativity of the psyche as magic, and rightly so, for it transforms reality and will always do so.

The basic archetypal image of this creatively transformed reality of the world is the self-contained rolling wheel of eternity, every single point of which is a "turning point," that "often concludes with beginning and starts with the end." For one of the paradoxes of life is that in its creative reality it is "existence" as pure present, but that the entire past flows into this existence while all the future flows out of it like a spring: hence it is a point both turning and at rest. This point of existence, the creative zero point of mysticism,[29] is a hiatus in creation, at which consciousness and the unconscious momentarily become a creative unity and a third term, a part of the one reality that almost "lingers" in the rapture and beauty of the creative moment.

But the poem continues:

28. George Thomson, *The Prehistoric Aegean*, p. 435.
29. See my "Mystical Man."

Every happy space ... is child or grandchild of parting.

That is to say, the place of being created in the world, even the happiest part of it, is built upon a parting, a departure from the eternity of the perfect circle into limitation and into a historical reality of past, present, and future—of generations. Here death creates separation and space and can only be overcome in the creative moment. And to pass in wonderment through creation is to incur the deadliness of separation, whereby all existence must be delimited over against the infinite. Thus every birth rests on death, just as all space rests on separation, and to be a child and grandchild is in every sense a beginning in which something else ends; but that which ends is at the same time a beginning, in which the past closes and is at the same time transcended. For in experiencing themselves as child and grandchild of separation, child and grandchild at the same time experience their birth from death and the rebirth in themselves of what is dead. They experience themselves as something created, that "often concludes with beginning and starts with the end."

But as they pass through creation in wonderment, the circuit transcends itself in a new turning. The circling wheel of birth and death, in which everything is at once beginning and end, is only the rim: the essential action in its center. And in this center appears the "transformed" Daphne. Fleeing from the pursuing god, escaping him by transformation, the soul becomes a laurel tree. Metamorphosed, she is no longer the pursued fugitive; her transformation is pure growth, but at the same time it is the laurel that crowns the poet as well as the pursuing god.

The flame at the beginning of the poem, in which the thing escapes by changing from enduring being to burning transformation, has its counterpart in the end; the eternally fugitive becomes a plant eternally rooted in being. In Apollo's love for Daphne, the pursuing god compels transformation; here again there is a creative sublimation of the soul, a higher love. For the Daphne who has escaped into the higher growth of her plant existence now feels "herself laurel." Now she is subject to the law and the love of Orpheus, of whom Rilke said: "Song is existence." [30]

Yet because it is existence, this higher existence of song, which captures the laurel-like soul, is not static but eternally moving. This creative spirit of song also "bloweth where it listeth." And although thàt which is consumed by the flame and that which pours forth in the spring were contained in the elementary nature of the creative, the soul transformed in the midst of this creation has become something other and higher. It is the partner of the divine song of which it is said: "A breath for nothing, A breathing in God, A Wind." Daphne, having taken root, desires only to be captivated; she desires only higher transformation—of herself, of God, of us.

> And Daphne, transformed,
> feeling herself laurel, wants you to change into wind.

30. *Die Sonette an Orpheus,* Erster Teil, III.

# LIST OF WORKS CITED

BARLACH, ERNST. *Ein selbsterzähltes Leben*. Berlin, 1928.

BUBER, MARTIN. *Die chassidischen Bücher*. Hellerau, 1928.

BUDGE, E. A. WALLIS. *The Gods of the Egyptians*. London, 1904. 2 vols.

BURCKHARDT, JAKOB. *The Civilization of the Renaissance in Italy*. Translated by S. G. C. Middlemore. London and New York, 1944.

DOUGLAS, R. LANGTON. *Leonardo da Vinci: His Life and His Pictures*. Chicago, 1944.

DU BOIS-REYMOND, F. "Über die archetypische Bedingtheit des erstgeborenen Sohnes und seiner Mutter." *Schweizerische Zeitschrift für Psychologie* (Berne), IX (1950).

EURIPIDES. *The Bacchae*. Translated by Gilbert Murray. London and New York, 1920.

FELDHAUS, FRANZ MARIA. *Leonardo der Techniker und Erfinder*. Jena, 1922.

FRÄNGER, WILHELM. *The Millennium of Hieronymus Bosch: Outlines of a New Interpretation*. Translated by Eithne Wilkins and Ernst Kaiser. London and New York, 1952.

FREEMAN, KATHLEEN. *Ancilla to the Pre-Socratic Philosophers*. Cambridge, Mass., and London, 1948.

FREUD, SIGMUND. *Leonardo da Vinci and a Memory of His Childhood*. In: The Standard Edition of the Complete Psychological Works of Sigmund Freud, translated by Alan Tyson, edited by James Strachey, Vol. XI. London, 1957.

HERZFELD, MARIE (ed.). *Leonardo da Vinci, der Denker, Forscher und Poet*. Leipzig, 1904; 4th edn., Jena, 1926.

HÖLDERLIN, JOHANN CHRISTIAN FRIEDRICH. *Hölderlin*. Translated by Michael Hamburger. New York, 1952.

HOLL, MORITZ. *Ein Biologe aus der Wende des XV Jahr-hundert: Leonardo da Vinci.* Graz, 1905.

HORAPOLLO. *The Hieroglyphics of Horapollo.* Translated and edited by George Boas. (Bollingen Series XXIII.) New York, 1950.

HUXLEY, ALDOUS. *The Doors of Perception.* London and New York, 1954.

*I Ching, or The Book of Changes.* Translated by Cary F. Baynes from the German translation of Richard Wilhelm. 3rd edn. (1 vol.) Princeton (Bollingen Series XIX) and London, 1967.

JAMES, WILLIAM. *The Varieties of Religious Experience.* New York, 1902.

JEREMIAS, ALFRED. *Handbuch der altorientalischen Geistes-kultur.* Leipzig, 1913; 2nd edn., Berlin and Leipzig, 1929.

JONES, ERNEST. *The Life and Work of Sigmund Freud,* Vol. II. New York, 1955.

JUNG, C. G. *Aion: Researches into the Phenomenology of the Self.* (Collected Works, Vol. 9, part ii.) New York and London, 1959.

———. "Picasso." In: *The Spirit in Man, Art, and Litera-ture.* Translated by R.F.C. Hull. (Collected Works, Vol. 15.) New York and London, 1966.

———. "Psychic Conflicts in a Child." In: *The Develop-ment of Personality.* Translated by R. F. C. Hull. (Col-lected Works, Vol. 17.) New York and London, 1954.

———. "A Psychological Approach to the Dogma of the Trinity." In: *Psychology and Religion: West and East.* Translated by R. F. C. Hull. (Collected Works, Vol. 11.) New York and London, 1958.

JUNG, C. G. *Psychological Types.* Translated by R.F.C. Hull. (Collected Works, Vol. 6.) Princeton and London, *1971*.

————. *Psychology and Alchemy.* Translated by R.F.C. Hull. (Collected Works, Vol. 12.) New York and London, 1953; 2nd edn., rev., 1968.

————. "The Relations between the Ego and the Unconscious." In: *Two Essays on Analytical Psychology.* Translated by R.F.C. Hull. (Collected Works, Vol. 7.) New York and London, 1953; 2nd edn., rev., 1966.

————. "A Review of the Complex Theory." In: *The Structure and Dynamics of the Psyche.* Translated by R.F.C. Hull. (Collected Works, Vol. 8.) New York and London, 1960.

————. *Symbols of Transformation.* Translated by R.F.C. Hull. (Collected Works, Vol. 5.) New York and London, 1956.

————. "Ulysses." In: *The Spirit in Man, Art, and Literature.* (Collected Works, Vol. 15.) New York and London, 1966.

———— and KERÉNYI, C. *Essays on a Science of Mythology.* Translated by R.F.C. Hull. New York (Bollingen Series XXII), 1949. (London edn., 1950, entitled *Introduction to a Science of Mythology.*)

KERÉNYI, C. *Asklepios: Archetypal Image of the Physician's Existence.* Translated by Ralph Manheim. (Archetypal Images in Greek Religion, 3.) New York (Bollingen Series LXV) and London, 1959.

————. "Kore." In: C. G. JUNG and KERÉNYI, *Essays on a Science of Mythology,* q.v.

KOCH, RUDOLF. *The Book of Signs*. Translated by Vyvyan Holland. London, 1930.

LANZONE, RIDOLFO VITTORIO. *Dizionario di mitologia egizia*. Turin, 1881–86.

LEO HEBRAEUS. *The Philosophy of Love (Dialoghi d'amore)*. Translated by F. Friedeberg-Seeley and Jean H. Barnes. London, 1937.

LEONARDO DA VINCI. *Literary Works*. See RICHTER, J. P.

———. *Notebooks*. See MACCURDY, EDWARD; RICHTER, IRMA A.

———. *Tout l'œuvre peint de Léonard de Vinci*. Introduction by Paul Valéry. Paris, 1950.

———. *Traktat von der Malerei (Trattato della Pittura)*. Edited by Marie Herzfeld. Jena, 1925.

*Life*. New York, July 17, 1939.

MACCURDY, EDWARD (ed.). *The Notebooks of Leonardo da Vinci*. London and New York, 1938. 2 vols.

MANN, THOMAS. *Dr. Faustus*. Translated by H. T. Lowe-Porter. New York, 1948; London, 1949.

MEREJKOWSKI, DMITRI. *The Romance of Leonardo da Vinci: The Forerunner*. Translated by Herbert Trench. New York and London, 1902.

NEUMANN, ERICH. *Amor and Psyche, the Psychic Development of the Feminine: A Commentary on the Tale by Apuleius*. Translated by Ralph Manheim. New York (Bollingen Series LIV) and London, 1956.

———. "Die Bedeutung des Erdarchetyps für die Neuzeit." *Eranos-Jahrbuch 1953* (Zurich, 1954).

———. *The Great Mother*. Translated by Ralph Manheim. New York (Bollingen Series XLVII) and London, 1955.

NEUMANN, ERICH. *Kulturentwicklung und Religion.* (Umkreisung der Mitte, I.) Zurich, 1953.

———. "Mystical Man." In: *The Mystic Vision.* Papers from the Eranos Yearbooks, 5. Princeton (Bollingen Series XXX) and London, 1969.

———. *The Origins and History of Consciousness.* Translated by R. F. C. Hull. New York (Bollingen Series XLII) and London, 1954.

———. "Die Psyche und die Wandlung der Wirklichkeitsebenen." *Eranos-Jahrbuch 1952* (Zurich, 1953).

———. *Depth Psychology and a New Ethic.* Translated by Eugene Rolfe. New York, 1969.

———. *Zur Psychologie des Weiblichen.* (Umkreisung der Mitte, II.) Zurich, 1953.

———. "Zur psychologischen Bedeutung des Ritus." *Eranos-Jahrbuch 1950* (Zurich, 1951). Also in *Kulturentwicklung und Religion,* q.v.

NIETZSCHE, FRIEDRICH WILHELM. "Peoples and Countries." Translated by J. M. Kennedy. In: *Complete Works,* edited by Oscar Levy, Vol. 13. Edinburgh and London, 1910.

OTTO, RUDOLF. "Spontanes Erwachen des sensus numinis." In: *Das Gefühl des Überweltlichen.* Munich, 1932.

PATER, WALTER. *The Renaissance: Studies in Art and Poetry.* London, 1924.

PFISTER, OSKAR. "Kryptolalie, Kryptographie und unbewusstes Vexierbild bei Normalen," *Jahrbuch für psychoanalytische und psychopathologische Forschungen* (Leipzig), V (1913).

PORTMANN, ADOLF. *Das Tier als soziales Wesen.* Zurich, 1953.

QUISPEL, GILLES. *Gnosis als Weltreligion.* Zurich, 1953.

RICHTER, IRMA A. (ed.). *Selections from the Notebooks of Leonardo da Vinci*. With commentaries. (The World's Classics.) London and New York, 1952.

RICHTER, JEAN PAUL (comp. and ed.). *The Literary Works of Leonardo da Vinci*. 2nd edn., New York and London, 1939. 2 vols.

RILKE, RAINER MARIA. *Correspondence in Verse with Erika Mitterer*. Translated by N. K. Cruikshank. London, 1953.

———. *Duineser Elegien. Die Sonette an Orpheus*. Zurich, 1951.

———. *Duino Elegies*. Translated by J. B. Leishman and Stephen Spender. London and New York, 1939.

———. "Die Sonette an Orpheus." In: *Gesammelte Werke*, III. Leipzig, 1930. Translated here by Ruth Speirs; unpublished.

———. "Die Worte des Herrn an Johannes auf Patmos." In: *Gedichte 1906–1926*. Wiesbaden, 1953. Translated here by J. M. Cohen; unpublished.

SCHILLER, JOHANN CHRISTOPH FRIEDRICH VON. "Über naive und sentimentale Dichtung." In: *Schillers Werke*. Edited by Arthur Kutscher. Vol. 9. Berlin, 1907.

SETHE, KURT HEINRICH (ed.). *Die alt-aegyptischen Pyramidentexte, nach den Papierabdrücken und Photographien des Berliner Museums*. Leipzig, 1908–22. 4 vols.

SIMENAUER, E. R. *Rainer Maria Rilke, Legende und Mythos*. Frankfurt a. M., 1953.

SPENGLER, OSWALD. *The Decline of the West*. Translated by Charles Francis Atkinson. New York, 1932. 2 vols. in 1.

[SPINOZA, BARUCH.] *Spinoza's Short Treatise on God, Man, and His Well-Being*. Translated by A. Wolf. London, 1910.

## LIST OF WORKS CITED

THOMSON, GEORGE. *The Prehistoric Aegean*. (Studies in Ancient Greek Society, Vol. I.) London, 1949.

TRITHEMIUS, JOHANNES. *De laudibus Sanctissimae Matris Annae tractatus*. Mainz, 1494.

VAILLANT, GEORGE C. *The Aztecs of Mexico*. (Penguin Books.) Harmondsworth, 1950.

VASARI, GIORGIO. *The Lives of the Painters*. Translated by A. B. Hinds. (Temple Classics.) London, 1900. 8 vols.

WILHELM, HELLMUT. *Change: Eight Lectures on the I Ching*. New York (Bollingen Series LXII) and London, 1960.

WILHELM, RICHARD. *Der Mensch und das Sein*. Jena, 1931.

WÖLFFLIN, HEINRICH. *Classic Art*. Translated by Peter and Linda Murray. London, 1952.

# INDEX

# INDEX

absolute, man and, 130
abstraction, 124
abyss, primeval, 13 & *n*
Africa, 129
Alberti, Leon Battista, 3
alchemy, 10, 61
alertness, 42, 43
anatomy, 35–6
ancestors, 11, 84
angels, and celestial
   world, 32
anima, 18, 19, 56, 182
animal(s), man and, 41;
   paintings, 86
animism, 123, 126
Anne, St., 44 & *n,* 55, 57–9,
   62, 63, 65, 66, 68, 72, 73,
   80, 190
antiquity, classical, 95
anxiety, 118
Apollo, 205
apperception, mythological,
   24
Apuleius, Lucius, 139
archetypes, 65, 82, 91–2,
   100–1, 105, 123, 124, 125,
   126, 140, 152, 153, 159,
   171–2, 178, 179, 180, 187,
   191; in creative man,
   17–8, 21–3, 94; and cultural canon, 16–7, 87,
   91–3, 107, 108; in dreams
   and fantasies, 10 & *n;*
   structure of, 34*n*

art, abstract, 124; and artist,
   90; Asian, 101; child's,
   118; deconcretization of,
   120; dehumanization of,
   119; demonic in, 123–4;
   eternal, 101; fragmenta-
   tion of, 117–8, 119–20; of
   insane, 118; irrational in,
   116, 118; and magic, 86;
   modern, 106, 112, 114,
   116–27, 133–4, 145, 166–7;
   naturalistic, 86, 95; nature
   and, 103; primitive, 101,
   118, 124, 137; realistic,
   94–5; religious, 104–5;
   styles, 84, 85; and time,
   81–134; timeless, 100,
   101; transcendence of,
   100–6; unity and, 91;
   world, 101
Artemis, 12
artist(s), 17–8, 97–8, 100,
   101-4, 169–70; and group,
   88, 90; as hero, 94; modern, 117–8, 124, 125,
   131–2
Asia, 131
atom bomb, 115, 121, 134
authority, 44–5
autumn, 155
Aztecs, 110, 129

Bacchus, 70–1, 72, 73
Bach, Johann Sebastian,

219

# ERICH NEUMANN

Born in Berlin in 1905, Erich Neumann earned his Ph.D. at the University of Berlin in 1927. He then began medical studies in Berlin and completed the examinations for the degree in 1933, after which he left Germany. He studied with C. G. Jung in 1934 and 1936, and from 1934 his permanent home was Tel Aviv, where he practiced as an analytical psychologist. For many years he returned regularly to Zurich to lecture at the C. G. Jung Institute. From 1948 until 1960 he was a regular contributor at the Eranos meetings in Ascona, Switzerland, and he also lectured frequently in England, France, and the Netherlands. He was a member of the International Association for Analytical Psychology and president of the Israel Association of Analytical Psychologists. He died in Tel Aviv on November 5, 1960.

Dr. Neumann had a theoretical and philosophical approach to analysis contrasting with the more clinical concern in England and the United States. His most valuable contribution to psychological theory is the empirical concept of "centroversion," a synthesis of extra- and introversion. His philosophical considerations of psychology are contained in *Depth Psychology and a New Ethic* (1949; tr. 1969), but he is best known for his statements of a coherent theory of feminine development. In *The Origins and History of Consciousness* (1949; tr. 1954), which illustrates by interpretations of basic mythologems the archetypal stages in the development of human consciousness, the emphasis on matriarchal symbolism foreshadowed his monumental work *The Great Mother* (first published in English, 1955), a study of the Magna Mater in the art of all times and in ethnological and mythological documents. Other works dealing with the idea of the feminine are *Amor and Psyche: The Psychic Development of the Feminine—A Commentary on the Tale by Apuleius* (1952; tr. 1956) and *The Archetypal World of Henry Moore* (first published in English, 1959). The extent of his interests and his penetrating comprehension of the fine arts are demonstrated by essays on Leonardo da Vinci, Marc Chagall, Mozart, Kafka, Georg Trakl, Jewish symbolism, and many other topics. Some of these are contained in his collected essays (*Umkreisung der Mitte*, 3 vols., 1953-54), four of which are translated in the present volume.

## DATE DUE